THE BEST
OF THE
GOOD
CLEAN
JOKES

BOB PHILLIPS

HARVEST HOUSE PUBLISHERS
EUGENE, OREGON

Cover by Dugan Design Group, Bloomington, Minnesota

Cover illustration © iStockphoto / zaricm

THE BEST OF THE GOOD CLEAN JOKES

Copyright © 1989 by Harvest House Publishers
Published by Harvest House Publishers
Eugene, Oregon 97402
www.harvesthousepublishers.com

ISBN 978-0-7369-5243-9 (pbk.)
ISBN 978-0-7369-5244-6 (eBook)

Printed in the United States of America

13 14 15 16 17 18 19 20 21 / BP-JH / 10 9 8 7 6 5 4 3 2 1

Aches and Pains

I've got so many aches and pains that if a new one comes today, it will be at least two weeks before I can worry about it.

Adam

Sam: My daddy has Washington's sword and Lincoln's hat.

Bill: My father has an Adam's apple.

■ ■ ■

Eve: Adam, do you love me?
Adam: Who else?

African Chieftain

An African chieftain flew to the United States to visit the president. When he arrived at the airport, a host of newsmen and television cameramen met him.

One of the reporters asked the chief if he had a comfortable flight.

The chief made a series of weird noises—"*Screech, scratch, honk, buzz, whistle, z-z-z-z*"—and then added in perfect English, "Yes, I had a very nice flight."

Another reporter asked, "Chief, do you plan to visit the Washington Monument while you're in the area?"

The chief made the same noises—"*Screech, scratch, honk, buzz, whistle, z-z-z-z*"—and then said, "Yes, and I also plan to visit the White House and the Capitol Building."

"Where did you learn to speak such flawless English?" asked the next reporter.

The chief replied, "*Screech, scratch, honk, buzz, whistle, z-z-z-z*—from the shortwave radio."

Agnostic

Q. What do you get if you cross an insomniac, an agnostic, and a dyslexic?

A. Someone who's up all night wondering if there is a dog.

Agreement

You can easily play a joke on a man who likes to argue—agree with him.

Airlines

A good-sized man approached the ticket counter at United Airlines and asked for a reservation from Los

Angeles to New York. The clerk knew that the plane was already filled with baggage and passengers.

"How much do you weigh, sir?" asked the clerk.

"With or without clothes?" the passenger asked.

"Well," said the clerk, "how do you intend to travel?"

Allowance

Son to father: About my allowance, Pop. It's fallen below the national average for teenagers.

Amen

The new Army recruit was given guard duty at two a.m. He did his best for a while, but about four a.m. he went to sleep. He awakened to find the officer of the day standing before him.

Remembering the heavy penalty for being asleep on guard duty, this smart young man kept his head bowed for another moment and then looked upward and reverently said, "Amen."

Amputated

Doctor: I have some good news and some bad news. Which do you want first?

Patient: Give me the bad news first.

Doctor: We amputated the wrong leg.

Patient: What is the good news?

Doctor: Your other leg doesn't need to be amputated after all.

Anger

A young girl who was writing a paper for school came to her father and asked, "Dad, what is the difference between annoyance, anger, and exasperation?"

The father replied, "It is mostly a matter of degree. Let me show you what I mean." With that the father pulled out his phone and dialed a number at random. To the man who answered the phone, he said, "Hello, is Melvin there?"

The man answered, "There's no one living here named Melvin. Why don't you learn to look up numbers before you dial?"

"See," said the father to his daughter. "That man was not a bit happy with our call. He was probably very busy with something, and we annoyed him. Now watch…"

The father dialed the number again. "Hello, is Melvin there?" he asked.

"Now look here!" came the heated reply. "You just called this number and I told you that there's no Melvin here! You've got a lot of nerve calling again!" The receiver slammed down hard.

The father turned to his daughter and said, "You see, that was anger. Now I'll show you what exasperation means." He again dialed the same number, and when a violent voice roared, "Hello!" the father calmly said, "Hello, this is Melvin. Have there been any calls for me?"

Another Doctor, Please

Looking down at a sick man, the doctor decided to tell him the truth. "I feel that I should tell you that you are a very sick man. I'm sure you would want to know the facts. I don't think you have much time left. Now, is there anyone you would like to see?"

Bending down toward his patient, the doctor heard him feebly answer yes.

"Who is it?"

In a slightly stronger tone, the patient said, "Another doctor."

Anyone—Please!

Boy: Why won't you marry me? Is there someone else?

Girl: There must be.

Apathy

The number one problem in our country is apathy—but who cares!

Applause

Applause before a boring speaker begins his talk is an act of faith.

Applause during the speech is an act of hope.

Applause after he has concluded is an act of charity.

Apple

A man traveling through the country stopped at a small fruit stand and bought some apples. When he commented that they were awfully small, the farmer replied, "Yup."

The man took a bite of one of the apples and exclaimed, "Not very flavorful, either."

"That's right," said the farmer. "Good thing they're small, ain't it?"

■ ■ ■

While visiting a friend who was in the hospital, I noticed several pretty nurses, each of whom was wearing a pin designed to look like an apple. I asked one nurse what the pin signified.

"Nothing," she said with a smile. "It's just to keep the doctors away."

Argument

If you really want the last word in an argument, try saying, "I guess you're right."

Army

The first sergeant was holding a class on combat for his company. He said, "Smith, what would you do if you saw seven hundred enemy soldiers coming at you?"

Smith said, "I would shoot them all with my rifle."

The sergeant asked, "On the right you see four hundred enemy soldiers charging at you. What would you do?"

Smith said, "I would shoot them with my rifle."

The sergeant continued, "Okay! On your left, Smith, you notice a thousand enemy soldiers heading straight at you. What would you do?"

Smith answered again, "I would shoot them all with my rifle."

The sergeant yelled, "Just a minute, Smith. Where are you getting all those bullets?"

The soldier smiled and said, "The same place you're getting all those enemy soldiers."

Arthritis

Doctor: The check you gave me for my bill came back.

Patient: So did my arthritis!

Asylum

Late one night in the insane asylum, one inmate shouted, "I'm Napoleon!"

Another said, "How do you know?"

The first inmate said, "God told me."

Just then a voice from the next room shouted, "I did not."

Atheist

I once wanted to become an atheist, but I gave up the idea. They don't have any holidays.

■ ■ ■

Atheist: Do you honestly believe that Jonah spent three days and nights in the belly of a whale?

Preacher: I don't know, sir, but when I get to heaven I'll ask him.

Atheist: But suppose he isn't in heaven?
Preacher: Then you ask him!

. . .

The atheist cannot find God for the same reason that a thief cannot find a policeman.

Baby Brother

For weeks a six-year-old lad kept telling his first-grade teacher about the baby brother or sister that was expected at his house. One day the mother allowed the boy to feel the movements of the unborn child. The six-year-old was obviously impressed but made no comment.

After that, he stopped telling his teacher about the impending event. The teacher finally leaned down to the boy and said, "Tommy, whatever has become of that baby brother or sister you were expecting at home?"

Tommy burst into tears and confessed, "I think Mommy ate it!"

Baby Food

I finally figured out why babies suck their thumbs. I tried some of the baby food.

Bachelor

Nancy: What's your excuse for not being married?
Rich: I was born that way.

Backseat Driver

"Daddy, before you married Mommy, who told you how to drive?"

Bad Driver

Did you hear about the cheerful truck driver who pulled up at a roadside café in the middle of the night for a dinner stop? Halfway through his dinner, three wild-looking motorcyclists roared up with swastikas on their chests and helmets.

For no reason at all, they selected the truck driver as a target. One poured pepper over his head, another stole his apple pie, the third deliberately upset his cup of coffee. The truck driver never said a word—he just rose, paid his check, and exited.

"That truck driver sure ain't much of a fighter," sneered one of the invaders.

The girl behind the counter, peering out into the night, added, "He doesn't seem to be much of a driver either. He just ran his truck right over three motor-cycles."

Bad News

Good news: All of you slaves who are rowing will get an extra ration of rum with the noon meal.

Bad news: After lunch, the captain wants to go waterskiing.

Bad Situations

Talk about bad situations—just think about…

- A screen door on a submarine.
- A stowaway on a kamikaze plane.
- A teenager who parks in a dark alley with his girl and his horn gets stuck.
- A soup sandwich.
- A pilot who ejects from a helicopter.
- A Hindu snake charmer with a deaf cobra.

Bald

If a man is bald in front, he's a thinker. If he's bald in the back, he's a lover. If he's bald in front and back, he thinks he's a lover.

Banana

Man on a train: That is the ugliest baby I have ever seen!

Woman: Conductor! Conductor! This man has just insulted my baby!

Conductor: Now, ma'am, don't get mad. I'll get a drink of water for you and a banana for your monkey.

Bank

Credit manager: Do you have any money in the bank?

Loan applicant: Certainly.

Credit manager: How much?

Loan applicant: I don't know. I haven't shaken it lately.

Baptists

Q. When you have 50 people all of different opinions, what do you have?

A. A Baptist church.

Baseball

The Bible talks a lot about baseball. In the big inning, Eve stole first, Adam stole second, Gideon rattled the pitchers, Goliath was put out by David, and the prodigal son made a home run.

Bath

Buck: Were you ever married?

Glen: Yeah, but my wife ran away.

Buck: How did it happen?

Glen: She ran away when I was taking a bath.

Buck: I'll bet she waited years for the opportunity.

Beans Again

Husband: Beans again!

Wife: I don't understand it. You liked beans on Monday, Tuesday, and Wednesday, and now all of a sudden you don't.

Beautiful

My wife is just as beautiful today as when I married her 20 years ago. It just takes her longer.

Beauty Shop

Carl: My wife spent four hours in the beauty shop the other day.

Charles: Boy, that's a long time.

Carl: Yeah, and that was just for the estimate!

Behavior

Father: Do you think Junior's behavior will improve if we buy him a bicycle?

Mother: No, but it'll spread his behavior over a wider area.

Bestseller

If you think no evil, see no evil, and hear no evil, chances are you'll never write a bestselling novel.

Big Bucks

Three boys were talking about how much money their fathers made.

The lawyer's son said, "My father goes into court on a case and often comes home with fifteen hundred dollars."

The doctor's son said, "My father performs an operation and earns two thousand dollars."

The minister's son, determined not to be outdone,

said, "That's nothing. My father preaches for just twenty minutes on Sunday morning, and it takes four men to carry the money."

Big John

A very small, sickly-looking man was hired as a bartender. The saloon owner gave him a piece of advice. "Drop everything and run for your life if you ever hear that Big John is on his way to town."

Several months later, a cowhand rushed in shouting, "Big John is a-comin'," and he accidentally knocked the small bartender to the floor in his hurry to get out. Before the bartender had a chance to recover, a giant of a man with a black bushy beard rode into the saloon on a buffalo, using a rattlesnake for a whip. The man tore the swinging doors off their hinges, knocked over tables, and flung the snake into the corner. He then pounded his massive fist on the bar, splitting it in half as he ordered a drink. The bartender nervously pushed a bottle toward the man, who bit the top off the bottle and downed the contents in one gulp.

As the man turned to leave, the bartender asked if he would like another drink.

"I ain't got no time," the man roared. "Big John is a-comin'."

Big Liar

Stranger: Catch any fish?

Fisherman: Did I! I took thirty out of this stream this morning.

Stranger: Do you know who I am? I'm the game warden.

Fisherman: Do you know who I am? I'm the biggest liar in the country.

Big Story

"I'm really worried."

"Why?"

"Well, my wife read *A Tale of Two Cities*, and we had twins. Later she read *The Three Musketeers*, and we had triplets. Now she is reading *Birth of a Nation*!"

Bird Legs

A young college student stayed up all night studying for his zoology test. As he entered the classroom the next morning, he saw ten stands. Each one had a bird on it with a sack covering everything but its legs. The professor announced that the test would be to look at birds' legs and give each bird's common name, habitat, genus, species, and so on.

The student looked at each set of bird legs. They all looked the same to him. He began to get upset. He had stayed up all night studying, and now had to identify birds by their legs. The more he thought about it, the madder he got.

Finally, he could stand it no longer. He strode to the professor's desk and said, "What a stupid test! How could anyone tell the difference between birds by looking at their legs?" With that the student threw his test on the professor's desk and walked out the door.

The class was so big, the professor didn't know the student's name, so he called out, "Excuse me...what's your name?"

The enraged student pulled up his pant legs and said, "You guess, buddy!"

Birthday

Husband to wife: "How do you expect me to remember your birthday when you never look any older?"

Birthstone

Son: Dad, this magazine article says that my birthstone is the ruby. What is yours?

Father: The grindstone.

Blacksmith

A village blacksmith working at his open forge, hammering a white-hot horseshoe, had just finished the shoe and thrown it to the ground to cool.

The local wise guy walked in at that moment. He picked up the horseshoe but dropped it with a howl of pain.

"Pretty hot, eh?" asked the blacksmith.

"Naw," said the wise guy. "It just don't take me long to look over a horseshoe."

Blame

To err is human; to blame it on the other guy is even more human.

Blank

A new preacher had just begun his sermon. He was a little nervous, and about ten minutes into the talk his mind went blank. He remembered what his seminary professors had taught him to do in a situation like this—repeat your last point. Often this would help you remember what is coming next. He decided to give it a try.

"Behold, I come quickly," he said. Still his mind was blank. He tried again. "Behold I come quickly!" Still nothing.

He tried it one more time with such force that he fell forward, knocking the pulpit to one side, tripping over a flowerpot, and falling into the lap of a little old lady in the front row.

The young preacher apologized and tried to explain what happened.

"That's all right, young man," said the little old lady. "It was my fault. I should have gotten out of the way. You told me three times you were coming!"

Blind

Two men were riding on a train for the first time. They brought bananas for lunch. Just as one of them bit into his banana, the train entered a tunnel.

First man: Did you take a bite of your banana?

Second man: No.

First man: Well, don't! I did and went blind!

Blue Ribbon

A minister from the city was filling the pulpit in a small farm community. After the service, he was invited to the house of one of the members for lunch. In the course of the conversation, he mentioned with pride that his son had won first prize in the 100 meter dash.

"I know just how you must feel," declared the member understandingly. "I remember how pleased I was last year when our pig won a blue ribbon at the fair."

Bluff

Boy: If you refuse to be mine, I'll hurl myself off that 500-foot cliff over there.

Girl: That's a lot of bluff.

Blunder

Mark Twain was once asked the difference between a mistake and a blunder. He explained it this way: "If you walk into a restaurant and walk out with someone's silk umbrella and leave your own cotton one, that is a mistake. But if you pick up someone's cotton umbrella and leave your own silk one, that's a blunder."

The Book of Parables

Recently I asked a man what his favorite book of the Bible was. He said, "The New Testament." I replied, "What part of the New Testament?" He said, "Oh, by far, I love the book of Parables best." I asked, "Would you kindly relate one of those parables to me?"

He said, "Once upon a time, a man went from Jerusalem to Jericho and fell among thieves. The thieves threw him into the weeds, and the weeds grew up and choked that man. He then went on and met the Queen of Sheba, and she gave that man a thousand talents of gold and silver and a hundred changes of raiment. He then got in his chariot and drove furiously to the Red Sea. When he got there, the waters parted, and he drove to the other side.

"On the other side, he drove under a big olive tree, got his hair caught on a limb, and was left hanging there. He hung there many days and many nights, and the ravens brought him food to eat and water to drink. One night while he was hanging there asleep, his wife Delilah came along and cut off his hair, and he dropped onto stony ground. The children of a nearby city came out and said, 'Go up, thou baldhead, go up, thou baldhead.' The man cursed the children, and two she bears came out of the woods and tore up the children.

"Then it began to rain, and it rained for forty days and forty nights. And he went and hid himself in a cave. Later he went out and met a man and said, 'Come and take supper with me.' But the man replied, 'I cannot come, for I have married a wife.' So he went out into the highways and byways and compelled them to come in, but they would not heed his call.

"He then went on to Jericho and blew his trumpet seven times, and the city walls came tumbling down. As he walked by one of the damaged buildings in the city, he saw Queen Jezebel sitting high up in a window, and when she saw him she laughed and made fun of him.

The man grew furious and said, 'Toss her down.' And they did. Then he said, 'Toss her down again.' And they did. They threw her down seventy times seven. And the fragments they gathered up were twelve baskets full. The question now is, whose wife will she be on the day of resurrection?"

Bore

A bore is someone who goes on talking while you're interrupting.

■ ■ ■

Mark Twain was once trapped by a bore who lectured to him about the hereafter: "Do you realize that every time I exhale, some poor soul leaves this world and passes on to the great beyond?"

Twain replied, "Really? Have you tried chewing cloves?"

Brain Food

Student: I hear that fish is brain food.
Roommate: Yeah, I eat it all the time.
Student: Well, there goes another theory.

Brains

Ike: How long can a man live without brains?
Mike: I don't know. How old are you?

■ ■ ■

Father: Do you think our son gets all his brains from me?

Mother: Probably. I still have all mine.

■ ■ ■

Don: She's a bright girl—she has brains enough for two.

Art: Then she's just the girl for you.

Breath

Sam: I can't catch my breath!

Pam: With your breath, you should be thankful.

Busy

Regardless of how busy people are, they are never too busy to stop and talk about how busy they are.

Cain

Heckler: Who was Cain's wife?

Preacher: I respect any seeker of knowledge, but I want to warn you, don't be tempted by too much inquiring after other men's wives.

Cake

Wife: Darling, you know that cake you asked me to bake for you? Well, the dog ate it.

Husband: That's okay, dear. I'll buy you another dog.

Camel

Q. What do you call a camel without a hump?
A. Humphrey.

■ ■ ■

Noah was standing at the gangplank, checking off the pairs of animals, when he saw three camels trying to get on board.

"Wait a minute!" said Noah. "Two each is the limit. One of you will have to stay behind."

"It won't be me," said the first camel. "I'm the camel whose back is broken by the last straw."

"I'm the one people swallow while straining at a gnat," said the second.

"I," said the third, "am the one that can pass through the eye of a needle sooner than a rich man can enter heaven."

"Come on in," said Noah. "The world is going to need all of you."

Can You Top This?

"My ancestry goes all the way back to Alexander the Great," said one lady. "And how far does your family go back?"

"I don't know," the second lady replied. "All of our records were lost in the Flood."

Can't Swim

A hunter shot a duck, and it fell into the lake. Quickly, he commanded his brand-new dog to retrieve the bird. The hound ran to the edge of the water, sniffed, and walked out on the lake. The hunter was amazed. He shot another duck, and it too fell into the lake. Again the hound walked out on the water to retrieve the duck before it sank. At last, the hunter thought, he had something to show his friend who never let anything get to him.

The next day the hunter suggested to his friend that they go do a little duck hunting. His friend shot a duck, and it fell into the lake. The dog walked across the water to retrieve it and drop it at the shooter's feet.

The hunter asked his friend, "What do you think of my bird dog?"

"I noticed he can't swim."

Car

Son: Dad, the Bible says that if you don't let me have the car, you hate me.

Dad: Where does it say that?

Son: Proverbs 13:24—"He that spareth his rod hateth his son."

Car Keys

The other day I was playing golf and saw an unusual thing. A golfer became so mad that he threw his brand-new set of golf clubs into the lake. A few minutes later he came back, waded into the lake, and retrieved his clubs. He took his car keys out of the bag and then threw the clubs back into the water.

Cat Food

A butcher was waiting on one woman when a second woman ran into the shop. "Quick," the second woman said to the butcher, "give me a pound of cat food please." Then she turned to the woman who had been ahead of her at the counter. "I hope you don't mind my butting in ahead of you," she said.

"No," said the first woman, "not if you're that hungry."

Cemetery Plot

"What did you give your wife for Christmas last year?"

"A cemetery plot."

"What are you going to give her this year?"

"Nothing. She didn't use last year's gift."

Chalk

One day I had a dream about my friend. I dreamed that he died and went to heaven. But to reach heaven, he had to climb a ladder. As he climbed, he was supposed to take a piece of chalk and make a mark on each rung for each sin he had committed.

As I looked in my dream I saw him coming back down the ladder. I asked him what he was doing. He said he was coming down for more chalk.

Change the Rope

An old European monastery is perched high on a 500-foot cliff. Visitors ride up in a big basket, pulled to the top with a ragged old rope.

Halfway up, a passenger nervously asked, "How often do you change the rope?"

The monk in charge replied, "Whenever the old one breaks."

Check

A young college student wrote, "Dear Mom and Dad, I haven't heard from you in nearly a month. Please send a check so I'll know you're all right."

Cheerful Giver

Hoping to develop his son's character, a father gave his son a penny and a quarter as he was leaving for Sunday school. "Now, Bill, you put whichever one you want in the offering plate," he said.

When the boy returned, his father asked which coin he had given. Bill answered, "Well, just before they sent around the plate, the preacher said, 'The Lord loves a cheerful giver.' I knew I could give the penny a lot more cheerfully than I could give the quarter, so I did."

Chess

A man dropped in to pay a friend an unexpected visit and was amazed to find him playing chess with a dog. The man watched in silence for a few minutes and then burst out, "That's the most incredible dog I ever saw in my life!"

"Oh, he isn't so smart," the friend answered. "I've beaten him three games out of four."

Chew with Your Mouth Closed

Hal: He's such a great speaker. I'd rather hear him speak than eat.

Cal: Me too. I've heard him eat.

The Chief Hog

A church secretary answered the phone and heard the caller say, "I want to talk to the chief hog of the trough."

"Sir," she replied, "that's no way to talk about the Reverend. He is the pastor of this church."

"Sorry, ma'am," he said, "I just wanted to donate a hundred thousand dollars to the church."

Quickly she said, "Just a minute. Here comes the fat pig now."

Children

Mother: Get your little brother's hat out of that mud puddle.

Son: I can't, Ma. He's got it strapped too tight under his chin.

▪ ▪ ▪

Father: Why are you always at the bottom of your class?

Son: What difference does it make? They teach the same thing at both ends.

▪ ▪ ▪

Mother: Suzie, what have you been doing this morning while I was working in the kitchen?

Suzie: I was playing postman.

Mother: How could you play postman when you don't have any letters?

Suzie: I was looking through your trunk in the garage and found a packet of letters tied with a nice ribbon, and I posted one in everyone's mailbox on the block.

Chips

A man arrested for gambling came before the judge. "We weren't playing for money," he explained to the judge. "We were just playing for chips."

"Chips are just the same as money," the judge sternly replied. "I fine you fifteen dollars."

The defendant looked sad, then slowly reached into his pocket and handed the judge three blue chips.

Chop to the Ego

Jerry: Whatever I say goes.

Terry: Then why don't you talk about yourself for a while?

Christmas

There's nothing like the Christmas season to put a little bounce in your checks.

■ ■ ■

A famous writer once sent Christmas cards containing nothing but 25 letters of the alphabet. When some of his friends admitted they didn't understand his message, he pointed to the card and said, "Look—no L!"

Church

"If absence makes the heart grow fonder," said a minister, "a lot of folks must love our church."

■ ■ ■

Wife: Did you see that hat Mrs. Jones wore to church?

Husband: No.

Wife: Did you see the new dress Mrs. Smith had on?

Husband: No.

Wife: Did you see Mrs. Davis's hat?

Husband: No.

Wife: A lot of good it does you to go to church!

Church Members

First pastor: I hear you had a revival.

Second pastor: Yes, we did.

First pastor: How many additions did you have?

Second pastor: We didn't have any additions, but we had some blessed subtractions.

Clean It Up

Q. If a man crosses the ocean twice without taking a bath, what is he called?

A. A dirty double-crosser.

Coach

A coach was being congratulated on receiving a lifetime contract. "I guess it's all right," he said. "But I remember another guy with a lifetime contract. He had a bad year, and the president called him in, pronounced him dead, and fired him."

College Cheer

The check from home.

Colonel Sanders

A farmer vows he increased egg production by putting this sign in the henhouse: "An egg a day keeps Colonel Sanders away."

Comfortable

The quickest way for a parent to get a child's attention is to sit down and look comfortable.

Commence Vacation

A traveling salesman was held up in the West by a storm and flood. He texted his office in New York: "Delayed by storm. Send instructions."

His boss texted back: "Commence vacation immediately."

Committee

A congregation was about to build a new church. The building committee, in consecutive meetings, passed the following resolutions:

1. We shall build a new church.

2. The new building is to be located on the site of the old one.

3. The material in the old building is to be used in the new one.

4. We shall continue to use the old building until the new one is completed.

Competition

Two barber shops were in red-hot competition. One put up a sign advertising haircuts for $5. His competitor put up one that read, "We repair $5 haircuts."

Complaint

Waiter: We haven't had a complaint in 25 years.

Customer: No wonder. The customers all starve to death before they're served.

■ ■ ■

Customer: I'll have some raw oysters, not too small, not too salty, not too fat. They must be cold, and I want them quickly!

Waiter: Yes, sir. With or without pearls?

Complete Protection

Watching the television news, we find that our highways aren't safe, our streets aren't safe, our parks aren't safe…but under our arms we've got complete protection.

Compliment

Whenever a man's friends begin to compliment him about looking young, he may be sure that they think he is growing old. —Washington Irving

Computer

If computers get too powerful, we can organize them into committees. That'll do them in.

Concentrate

Member: Pastor, how did you get that cut on your face?

Pastor: I was thinking about my sermon this morning and cut myself shaving.

Member: That's too bad! Next time you should concentrate on your shaving and cut your sermon!

Conclusion

He needs no introduction. What he needs is a conclusion.

■ ■ ■

Recruit: What if my parachute doesn't open?

Instructor: That's what we call jumping to a conclusion.

. . .

Jumping to conclusions is not half as much exercise as digging for facts.

Cook

Bride: The two things I cook best are meat loaf and apple dumplings.

Groom: Great! Which is this?

Cookies

Wife: I baked two kinds of cookies today. Would you like to take your pick?

Husband: No thanks. I'll use my hammer.

Cover-Up

In the beginning God created all men bald. Later He became ashamed of some and covered them up with hair.

Crazy

Psychiatrist to patient: "If you think you're walking out of here cured after only three sessions, you're crazy!"

Credit

Glen: Are you still living within your income?

Rich: No. It's all I can do to live within my credit.

Crib

One night a wife found her husband standing over their baby's crib. Silently she watched him. As he stood looking down at the sleeping infant, she saw a mixture of emotions on his face: disbelief, doubt, delight, amazement, enchantment, skepticism.

Touched by this unusual display and the deep emotions it aroused, with eyes glistening she slipped her arm around her husband. "A penny for your thoughts," she said.

"It's amazing!" he replied. "I just can't see how anybody can make a crib like that for only fifty bucks."

Crime

We don't seem to be able to check crime, so why not legalize it and then tax it out of business? —Will Rogers

Crossword Puzzle

Did you hear about the crossword puzzle addict who died and was buried six feet down and three feet across?

Cupid

Cupid's dart hurts more coming out than going in.

Curiosity

A sharp nose indicates curiosity. A flattened nose indicates too much curiosity.

Cyclone

A Kansas cyclone hit a farmhouse just before dawn one morning. It lifted the roof off, picked up the bed on which the farmer and his wife slept, and set it down gently in the next county.

The wife began to cry.

"Don't be scared, Mary," her husband said. "We're not hurt."

Mary continued to cry. "I'm not scared," she responded between sobs. "I'm happy—this is the first time in fourteen years we've been out together."

Damp

Pam: Why was your letter so damp?
Rosie: Postage dew, I guess.

Dance

Rod: I'm through with that girl.
Doug: Oh, why?
Rod: She asked me if I danced.
Doug: Well, what's wrong with that?
Rod: I was dancing with her when she asked me.

Darling

A sorely pressed newlywed sought valiantly to console his bride, who sprawled, dissolved in tears, on the chaise lounge. "Darling," he implored, "believe me. I never said you were a terrible cook. I merely pointed out that our garbage disposal has developed an ulcer."

Dead in Christ

One pastor said that the people in his church would be the first to go up in the rapture. He gave his reason: "The Bible says, 'The dead in Christ shall rise first.'"

Deaf

Stewardess: I'm sorry, Mr. Jones, but we left your wife behind in Chicago.

Man: Thank goodness! For a moment there I thought I was going deaf!

Deaf and Dumb

Hokum: Why do you tell everyone I'm deaf and dumb?

Yokum: That's not true. I never said you were deaf.

Dear John

One of Joe's bunk mates broke up with his girlfriend. The girlfriend sent him a note, demanding that he return her photograph immediately. The soldier borrowed a collection of several pictures of various girls and sent them to his ex-sweetheart with her photo tucked in among them. He enclosed a note:

"Dear Mildred, pick out yours. I forgot what you look like."

Deceive

PK: She said I'm interesting, brave, and intelligent.

Bob: You should never go steady with a girl who deceives you from the very start.

Deep Water

When you're in deep water, it's a good idea to keep your mouth shut.

Died

Pastor: Here is a plaque for the members who died in the service.

Man: Which one—morning or evening?

Diet

A diet is a short period of starvation preceding a gain of five pounds.

Diplomat

One who never heard that old joke before.

Disagree

By the time I found out my father was right, my son was old enough to disagree with me.

■ ■ ■

Wife: I'm afraid the mountain air would disagree with me.

Husband: My dear, it wouldn't dare.

Disbarred

If lawyers are disbarred and ministers unfrocked, perhaps electricians get delighted...Far Eastern diplomats disoriented...cashiers distilled...alpine climbers dismounted...piano tuners unstrung...orchestra leaders disbanded...artists' models deposed...cooks deranged...nudists redressed...office clerks defiled...mediums dispirited...dressmakers unbiased.

Discovered

A wife is the only person who can look into the top drawer of a dresser and find a man's socks that aren't there.

Disposition

They say brunettes have a sweeter disposition than blondes and redheads. Don't believe it! My wife has been all three, and I couldn't see any difference.

Distinguished

Reporter: And how did you win the Distinguished Service Medal?

Private: I saved the lives of my entire regiment.

Reporter: Wonderful! And how did you do that?

Private: I fired the cook.

Divorce

A couple in Hollywood got divorced and then got remarried. The divorce didn't work out.

■ ■ ■

Dopey: Why did the cow get a divorce?

Dopier: She got a bum steer.

Do Your Best

Judge: Thirty years in prison!

Defendant: But, Judge, I won't live that long!

Judge: Don't worry—do what you can.

Doctor

People who think that time heals everything haven't tried sitting it out in a doctor's waiting room.

■ ■ ■

Dr. Hanson: So the operation on the man was just in the nick of time?

Dr. Poure: Yes. In another twenty-four hours he would have recovered.

■ ■ ■

Patient: My tongue tingles when I touch it to a cracked walnut wrapped in used toaster-oven aluminum foil—what's wrong with me?

Doctor: You have far too much free time.

■ ■ ■

Doctor: Nurse, how is that little boy doing—the one who swallowed ten quarters?

Nurse: No change yet.

Dopey Blonde

Marge: What happened to that dopey blonde your husband used to run around with?

Eileen: I dyed my hair!

Double Take

Life's briefest moment is the time between reading the sign on the freeway and realizing you just missed your exit.

Doughnut

Customer: Waitress, why is my doughnut all smashed?

Waitress: You said you wanted a cup of coffee and a doughnut—and step on it.

Down with the Ship

A soldier who lost his rifle was reprimanded by his captain and told he would have to pay for it.

"Sir," gulped the soldier, "suppose I lost a tank. Surely I would not have to pay for that!"

"Yes, you would," bellowed the captain. "Even if it took the rest of your life."

"Well," said the soldier, "now I know why the captain goes down with his ship."

Dragon Milk

Q. How do you get dragon milk?
A. From a cow with short legs.

Driving

Driving instructor: What would you do if you were going up an icy hill and the motor stalled and the brakes failed?

Student: I'd quickly adjust the rearview mirror.

Drums

Mother: I don't think the tenant upstairs likes Mike to play his drums.

Father: Why do you say that?

Mother: He just gave Mike a knife and asked him if he knew what was inside them.

Dryer

A sign on a dryer in a coin laundry reads, "This dryer is worthless." A sign on the next dryer reads, "This dryer is next to worthless."

Dull

The trouble with telling a good story is that it reminds someone else of a dull one.

■ ■ ■

One girl to another: "There's never a dull moment when you're out with Wilbur…it lasts the whole evening."

Dumb Question

Fred: Did you fall down the elevator shaft?

George: No, I was sitting here and they built it around me.

Dust

On the way home from church a little boy asked his mother, "Is it true, Mommy, that we are made of dust?"

"Yes, darling."

"And do we go back to dust again when we die?"

"Yes, dear."

"Well, Mommy, when I said my prayers last night and looked under the bed, I found someone who is either coming or going."

Dying

Pete was very close to dying but made a miraculous recovery. His pastor came to visit him in the hospital.

"Tell me, Pete. When you were so near death's door, did you feel afraid to meet your Maker?"

"No, Pastor," Pete answered. "It was the other man I was afraid of!"

Dynamite

You know, if brains were dynamite, he wouldn't have enough to blow his nose!

Earache

A woman complained of an earache, so her doctor examined her and found a piece of string dangling from her right ear. The doctor began pulling it out, and the more he pulled, the more string came out.

Suddenly the pulling became harder, and he struggled with the string. To his amazement, out fell a bouquet of roses.

The doctor exclaimed, "Good gracious, where did this come from?"

"How should I know?" said the woman. "Why don't you look at the card?"

Earplugs

There is a new cigarette with earplugs in every pack. It's for people who don't want to hear why they should quit smoking.

Earthquake

A recent earthquake frightened the inhabitants of a nearby town. One couple sent their little boy to stay with an uncle in another city, explaining the reason for the nephew's sudden visit. A day later the parents received this note: "Am returning your boy. Send the earthquake."

Eating

Doctors say that if you eat slowly, you eat less. You certainly will if you are a member of a large family.

Eggs

Q. Which came first, the chicken or the egg?
A. The chicken, of course. God couldn't lay an egg.

■ ■ ■

Teacher: Why don't you brush your teeth? I can see what you had for breakfast this morning.
Student: What did I have?
Teacher: Eggs!
Student: Nope—that was yesterday.

Egress

It is said that P.T. Barnum, the famed circus magnate, hung a large sign over one of the exits of his museum that read, "This way to the egress." Many people in the crowds, eager to see what an egress looked like, passed through the door and found themselves out on the street.

Elephant Ears

Customer: Your sign says, "$50 to anyone who orders something we can't furnish." I would like to have an elephant-ear sandwich.

Waiter: Ohhh…we're going to have to pay you the $50.

Customer: No elephant ears, huh?

Waiter: Oh, we've got lots of them, but we're all out of those big buns!

Elephants

Q. Why do elephants have flat feet?
A. From jumping out of trees.

■ ■ ■

Q. Why is it dangerous to go into the jungle between two and four in the afternoon?
A. Because that's when elephants are jumping out of trees.

■ ■ ■

Q. Why are pygmies so small?
A. They went into the jungle between two and four in the afternoon.

Embarrassing

Nothing is as embarrassing as watching your boss do something you assured him couldn't be done.

Empire State Building

Did you hear about the man who jumped from the Empire State Building and lived to tell about it? He told the people on the ninety-third floor, those on the eighty-fourth floor, everyone on the sixty-second floor…

Empty Space

Debby: I have a cold or something in my head.
Beth: I bet it's a cold.

Ends

Why is it that every time you start to make ends meet, somebody comes along and moves the ends?

Endure

First church member: That sermon reminded me of the peace of God—it passed all understanding.

Second member: It reminded me of the mercies of God—I thought it would endure forever.

Enemies

The Bible tells us to love our neighbors and also to love our enemies, probably because they are generally the same people.

Engagement Ring

Mary: Well, what happened when you showed the girls in the office your new engagement ring? Did they all admire it?

Sara: Better than that—four of them recognized it.

Entrance to Sale

Business was pretty bad at Max's Bargain Emporium. Then, to compound Max's troubles, Harry's on his right decided to run a big going-out-of-business sale and hung up a sign that said, THE GREATEST GOING-OUT-OF-BUSINESS SALE EVER. YOU COULDN'T GET BIGGER BARGAINS IF WE WERE REALLY GOING OUT OF BUSINESS.

Then Leo's, on Max's left, decided to run a sale and hung up this sign: FIRE SALE. YOU COULDN'T GET BETTER BUYS EVEN IF THERE WAS A REAL FIRE.

Max joined the fun. He hung up a sign directly between the others reading: ENTRANCE TO SALE.

Escape

The news media featured a convict's daring daylight escape from prison and his voluntary return and surrender later that evening. When reporters asked him why he had come back, he said, "The minute I sneaked home to see my wife, the first thing she said was, 'Where have you been? You escaped eight hours ago!'"

Excellent Time

The loudspeaker of the big jet clicked on, and the captain's voice announced in a clear, even tone, "Ladies and gentlemen, there's no cause for alarm, but you should know that for the last three hours we've been flying without the benefit of radio, compass, radar, or navigational beam due to the breakdown of certain key components. This means that we are lost and are not quite sure in which direction we are heading. I'm sure you'll be glad to know, however, that we're making excellent time."

Excuse Me

A meek little man in a restaurant timidly touched the arm of a man putting on an overcoat. "Excuse me," he said, "but do you happen to be Mr. Smith of Newport?"

"No, I'm not!" the man answered impatiently.

"Oh…er…well…" stammered the first man, "you see, I am, and that's his overcoat you're putting on."

Experience

Experience is the thing you have left when everything else is gone.

■ ■ ■

A young man came to interview a bank president. "Tell me, sir, how did you become so successful?"

"Two words: right decisions."

"How do you make right decisions?"

"One word: experience."

"And how do you get experience?"

"Two words: wrong decisions."

Eye Sore

Patient: Every time I have a cup of coffee, I get a stabbing pain in my right eye. What should I do?

Doctor: Take the spoon out of your cup.

Face

If your face is your fortune, you won't have to pay any income tax.

. . .

Jill: Your face would stop a clock.
Kim: And yours would make one run!

. . .

The popular preacher Charles Spurgeon was admonishing a class of divinity students on the importance of making their facial expressions harmonize with their speech when preaching. "When you speak of heaven," he said, "let your face light up and be irradiated with a heavenly gleam. Let your eyes shine with reflected glory. And when you speak of hell...well, then your everyday face will do."

False

Q. What do we call the last teeth to appear in the mouth?
A. False.

Family Tree

The cheapest way to have your family tree traced is to run for a public office.

Famous Last Words

"You can make it easy—that train isn't coming fast."

"Gimmee a match. I think my gas tank is empty."
"Wife, these biscuits are tough."
"Let's see if it's loaded."
"Step on her, boy, we're only going seventy-five."
"Just watch me dive from that bridge."
"If you knew anything, you wouldn't be a traffic cop."
"Lemme have that bottle; I'll try it."
"What? Your mother is going to stay another month?"
"Say, who's boss of this place, anyhow?"

Fans

Q. What makes a baseball stadium cool?
A. The fans.

A Few Pounds

Wife: Honey, will you still love me after I put on a few pounds?

Husband: Yes, I do.

Fiddle Around

When Joe was a little boy, he took fiddle lessons. One day while he was practicing, scraping dismally back and forth with his bow, his dog started wailing and howling. Finally Joan, who was trying to do her homework, stuck her head into the room where her brother was practicing.

"For goodness' sake!" she complained. "Can't you play something the dog doesn't know?"

Fine

A fine is a tax for doing wrong. A tax is a fine for doing well.

. . .

I'm fine, I'm fine.
There's nothing whatever the matter with me.
I'm just as healthy as I can be.
I have arthritis in both of my knees,
And when I talk, I talk with a wheeze.
My pulse is weak and my blood is thin,
But I'm awfully well for the shape I'm in.
My teeth eventually will have to come out,
And I can't hear a word unless you shout.
I'm overweight, and I can't get thin,
But I'm awfully well for the shape I'm in.
Arch supports I have for both my feet
Or I wouldn't be able to walk down the street.
Sleep is denied me every night,
And every morning I'm really a sight.
My memory is bad and my head's a-spin,
And I practically live on aspirin,
But I'm awfully well for the shape I'm in.
The moral is, as this tale unfolds,
That for you and me who are growing old,
It's better to say "I'm fine" with a grin
Than to let people know the shape we're in!

Finished

A man is incomplete until he's married…then he's finished.

■ ■ ■

A little boy in church, awaking after a nap, asked his father, "Has the preacher finished?"

"Yes, son, he has finished…but he hasn't stopped."

First Baby

The phone rang in the maternity ward, and an excited voice on the other end said, "This is George Smith, and I'm bringing my wife in—she's about to have a baby!"

"Calm down," replied the attendant. "Tell me, is this her first baby?"

"No," the voice replied, "this is her husband."

Fish

A fisherman had two sons named Toward and Away. Every day he would go fishing and return late at night, always talking about the giant fish he had almost caught. One day he took Toward and Away fishing with him.

That night he returned home more excited than ever.

"Sally," he yelled to his wife, "you should have seen the fish I saw today. A tremendous gray fish, ten feet long with horns and fur all over its back. It had legs like a caterpillar. It came crawling out of the water, snatched our son Toward, and swallowed him in one gulp!"

"Good gracious!" exclaimed his wife. "That's horrible!"

"Oh, that was nothing," said her husband. "You should have seen the one that got Away!"

Five Hundred Times

In the traffic court of a large Midwestern city, a young lady was brought before the judge because of a ticket given her for driving through a red light. She explained to the judge that she was a schoolteacher and requested an immediate disposal of her case so that she could hurry to her classes.

A wild gleam came into the judge's eye. "You're a schoolteacher? Ma'am, I've waited years to have a schoolteacher in this court. Sit down at that table and write 'I went through a red light' five hundred times!"

Flashlight

A boy from New York was being led through the swamps of Georgia.

"Is it true," he asked, "that an alligator won't attack you if you carry a flashlight?"

"That depends," replied the guide, "on how fast you carry the flashlight."

Flirt

Sally: I wonder what's wrong with that tall blond guy over there. Just a minute ago he was getting awful friendly, and then all of a sudden he turned pale, walked away, and won't even look at me anymore.

Linda: Maybe he saw me come in. He's my husband.

Flirting

The minister arose to address his congregation. "There is a certain man among us today who is flirting with another man's wife. Unless he puts twenty dollars in the offering, his name will be read from the pulpit."

When the collection plate came in, there were several $20 bills and a $10 bill with this note attached: "Other ten on payday."

Foiled Again

Q. What did the man say when he lost the fencing match?

A. Foiled again.

Fool

Reverend Henry Ward Beecher entered Plymouth Church one Sunday and found several letters awaiting him. He opened one and found it contained a single word—"Fool." Quietly and with becoming seriousness, he addressed the congregation.

"I have known many an instance of a man writing a letter and forgetting to sign his name, but this is the only instance I have ever known of a man signing his name and forgetting to write the letter."

Football

The pastor of the Calvary Baptist Church in Tulsa calls this his "football theology":

Draft choice: Selection of a pew near to (or away from) air-conditioning vents.

Bench warmer: Inactive member.

In the pocket: Where too many Christians keep their tithes.

Fumble: Lousy sermon.

Two-minute warning: Deacon in front row taking a peek at his watch in full view of the preacher.

Forgetful

"George is so forgetful," the sales manager complained to his secretary. "It's a wonder he can sell anything. I asked him to pick up some sandwiches for me on his way back from lunch, and I'm not sure he'll even remember to come back."

Just then the door flew open, and in bounced George. "You'll never guess what happened!" he shouted. "While I was at lunch, I met Old Man Brown, who hasn't bought anything from us for five years. Well, we got to talking and he gave me a half-million-dollar order!"

"See," sighed the sales manager to his secretary. "I told you he'd forget the sandwiches."

Fortune

Wife to husband who just got off the pennyweight scale: "Your fortune says you are handsome, debonair, and wealthy. It even has your weight wrong!"

Four to Go

Sue: See that woman over there? She's been married four times—first to a millionaire, then to an actor, then to a minister, and last to an undertaker.

Sal: I know! One for the money, two for the show, three to get ready, and four to go!

Four Types of Ministers

Ministers fall into four categories:

1. Those who do not have any notes, and the people have no idea how long they will speak.

2. Those who put down on the podium in front of them each page of their sermon as they read it. These honest ones enable the audience to keep track of how much more is to come.

3. Those who cheat by putting each sheet of notes under the others in their hand.

4. And worst of all, those who put down each sheet of notes as they read it and then horrify the audience by picking up the whole batch and reading off the other side.

Frugal

The man walked into the house panting and almost completely exhausted. "What happened, honey?" his wife asked.

"It's a great new idea I have," he gasped. "I ran all the way home behind the bus and saved two dollars."

"That wasn't very bright," replied his wife. "Why didn't you run behind a taxi and save ten bucks?"

■ ■ ■

A rather frugal man asked the bank for a loan of one dollar and was told he would have to pay 7 percent interest at the end of the year. For security he offered $60,000 in US bonds. The banker, foreseeing a potential depositor, accepted the bonds and gave the man a dollar.

At the end of the year, he was back with a dollar and seven cents to clear up his debt and ask for the return of his bonds. Upon returning the bonds, the banker asked, "I don't want to be inquisitive, but since you have all those bonds, why did you have to borrow a dollar?"

"Well," said the tightfisted old gent, "I really didn't have to. But do you know of any other way I could get a safety-deposit box for seven cents a year?"

Funeral

"Do you believe in life after death?" the boss asked one of his younger employees.

"Yes, sir."

"Well, that makes everything just fine," the boss went

on. "About an hour after you left yesterday to go to your grandfather's funeral, he stopped in to see you."

■ ■ ■

A young minister, in the first days of his first parish, was obliged to call on the widow of an eccentric man who had just died. Standing before the open casket and consoling the widow, he said, "I know this must be a very hard blow, Mrs. Vernon. But we must remember that what we see here is the husk only, the shell...the nut has gone to heaven."

Galaxies

NASA reports that galaxies are speeding away from earth at 90,000 miles a second. What do you suppose they know that we don't?

Garage Sale

A garage sale is a technique for distributing all the junk in your garage among all the other garages in the neighborhood.

Generation

The older generation thought nothing of getting up at five every morning—and the younger generation doesn't think much of it either.

George

A man in a supermarket was pushing a cart that contained, among other things, a screaming baby. As the man proceeded along the aisles, he kept repeating softly, "Keep calm, George. Don't get excited, George. Don't yell, George."

A lady watched with admiration and then said, "You are certainly to be commended for your patience in trying to quiet little George."

"Lady," he declared, "*I'm* George!"

Germs

Husband: Don't put that money in your mouth. There are germs on it.

Wife: Don't be silly. Even a germ can't live on the money you earn.

Getting Even

Judge: Haven't I seen you before?

Man: Yes, Your Honor. I taught your daughter how to play the piano.

Judge: Thirty years.

Ghost

A photographer went to a haunted castle determined to get a picture of a ghost that was said to appear only once in a hundred years.

Not wanting to frighten off the spook, the photographer sat in the dark until midnight, when the apparition became visible.

The ghost turned out to be friendly and consented to pose for a snapshot. The happy photographer popped a bulb into his camera and took the picture. Then he dashed to his studio, developed the negative…and groaned. It was underexposed and completely blank.

Moral: The spirit was willing but the flash was weak.

•••

The patient explained to the psychiatrist that he was haunted by visions of his departed relatives.

Patient: Ghosts are perched on the tops of fence posts around my garden every night. They just sit there and watch me and watch me and watch me. What can I do?

Psychiatrist: That's easy—just sharpen the tops of the posts.

Glass Eye

Christy: That lady has a glass eye.

Lisa: How did you find that out?

Christy: Oh, it just came out in the conversation.

Gnu

Mama Gnu was waiting for Papa Gnu as he came home for dinner one evening.

"Our little boy was very bad today," she declared. "I want you to punish him."

"Oh no," said Papa Gnu. "I won't punish him. You'll have to learn to paddle your own gnu."

Gold

A member of the Inca tribe was captured by the Spanish. The captain told his interpreter to say to the Inca Indian, "Tell him if he doesn't tell us where they have hidden all of their gold, we will burn both of his feet in the fire."

Through the interpreter the Inca Indian responded, "I'd rather die than tell you where the gold is." With that, they burned his feet in the fire.

The captain then told the interpreter to say, "Tell him that if he doesn't tell us where the gold is hidden, we will hang him from that noose on the tree over there."

The Inca Indian again responded, "I'd rather die than tell you where the gold is." With that, they took him over to the tree and hung him until he could hardly breathe.

The Spanish captain then ordered the Indian to be brought to him again. This time he said to the interpreter, "Tell him if he doesn't tell us where the gold is, we will skin him alive."

The Inca Indian could stand it no longer and said, "The gold is hidden in a little cave just behind the large waterfall. The waterfall is one mile over the hill to the right."

The interpreter turned to the captain and said, "He said he would rather die than tell you where the gold is."

Golf

Golf is a lot of walking, broken up by disappointment and bad arithmetic.

62

＊＊＊

A group of golfers were telling tall stories. At last came a veteran's turn. "Well," he said, "I once drove a ball, accidentally of course, through a cottage window. The ball knocked over an oil lamp, and the place caught on fire."

"What did you do?" asked his friends.

"Oh," said the veteran, "I immediately teed another ball, took careful aim, and hit the fire alarm on Main Street. The fire engine arrived before any major damage was done."

＊＊＊

Wife: George, you promised you'd be home at four. It's now eight.

George: Honey, listen to this—poor ol' Fred is dead. He just dropped over on the eighth green.

Wife: Oh, that's awful.

George: It surely was. For the rest of the round it was hit the ball, drag Fred, hit the ball, drag Fred…

＊＊＊

A distinguished clergyman and one of his parishioners were playing golf. It was a very close match, and at the last hole the clergyman teed up, addressed the ball, and swung his driver with great force. The ball, instead of sailing down the fairway, merely rolled off the tee and settled slowly about 12 feet away.

The clergyman frowned, glared, and bit his lip but said nothing. His opponent regarded him for a moment, and then remarked, "Pastor, that's the most profane silence I have ever witnessed."

Good

The man who says he is just as good as half the folks in the church seldom specifies which half.

A Good Day

The man of the house finally took all his family's disabled umbrellas to the repair shop. Two days later, on the way to his office, when he got up to leave the bus, he absentmindedly grabbed the umbrella belonging to a woman beside him. The women cried "Stop, thief!" and rescued her umbrella. The man felt ashamed and confused.

The same day, he stopped at the repair shop and received all eight of his umbrellas duly repaired. As he entered a bus with the unwrapped umbrellas tucked under his arm, he was horrified to see the lady of his morning adventure glaring at him. Her voice came to him charged with withering scorn: "Huh! Had a good day, didn't you!"

Good Deal

A man I know solved the problem of too many visiting relatives. He borrowed money from the rich ones and loaned it to the poor ones. Now none of them come back.

A Good Laugh

Tim: What would you say if I asked you to be my wife?"

Kim: Nothing. I can't talk and laugh at the same time."

Good News

Bad news: Your wife just ran off with your best friend.

Good news: That's two people off your Christmas list.

Good Old Days

Too many people keep looking back to the good old days:

1880…"I walked fourteen miles through snow and rain to go to school."

1915…"I had to walk five miles every day."

1936…"It was eleven blocks to the bus stop every morning."

1950…"I had to buy gasoline for my own car."

1966…"When I drove to school as a boy, we didn't have power brakes, power steering, or power windows."

Good Sport

The trouble with being a good sport is that you have to lose to prove it.

Good Thinking

"Your age, please?" asked the census taker.

"Well," said the woman, "let me figure it out. I was eighteen when I was married, and my husband was thirty. He is now sixty, or twice as old as he was then, so I am now thirty-six."

■ ■ ■

Panting and perspiring, two men on a tandem bicycle at last got to the top of a steep hill.

"That was a stiff climb," said the first man.

"It certainly was," replied the second man. "If I hadn't kept the brake on, we would have slid down backward."

Gorilla

A gorilla walked into a drugstore and ordered a $1 sundae. He put down a $10 to pay for it. The clerk thought, "What can a gorilla know about money?" So he handed back a single dollar in change.

As he did, he said, "You know, we don't get many gorillas in here."

"No wonder," answered the gorilla, "at nine dollars a sundae."

Gossip

"I think we need to change the morning hymn," said the minister to his song leader. "My topic this morning is gossip. I don't think 'I Love to Tell the Story' would be the best song."

■ ■ ■

First man: I think we should all confess our faults one to another. I've got a terrible habit of stealing.

Second man: I've got a terrible habit of lying.

Third man: I beat my wife.

Fourth man: When no one is around, I get drunk.

Fifth Man: I've got the terrible habit of gossiping. I can hardly wait to get out of here!

Grass Houses

Did you hear about the tribe in Africa that stole the king's throne from a rival tribe? They hid the throne in the rafters of their grass hut and then celebrated by having a party in the hut. Suddenly the rafters broke, and the throne fell down and killed all of the men.

The moral of the story is that those who live in grass houses shouldn't stow thrones.

Gray Hair

Mary: I wonder if my husband will love me when my hair is gray.

Carri: Why not? He's loved you through three shades already.

Grocery Money

Husband: What have you been doing with all the grocery money I gave you?

Wife: Turn sideways and look in the mirror.

Growing Older

An elderly gentleman wasn't feeling well and became irritated with his doctor because he wasn't getting better after five visits.

"Look!" said the doctor. "I'm doing all I can to help you. I can't make you younger."

"I wasn't particularly interested in getting younger," said the old man. "I just want to continue growing older."

Grumpy

Marriage counselor to female client: Have you been waking up grumpy in the morning?

Client: No, I always let him sleep.

Guardian Angel

Wife: Aren't you driving a little too fast, dear?

Husband: Don't you believe in a guardian angel? He'll take care of us.

Wife: Yes, I do. But I'm afraid we left him miles back!

Half-Wit

He spends half his time trying to be witty. You might say he's a half-wit.

Hanged

The applicant for life insurance was finding it difficult to fill out the application. The salesman asked what the trouble was, and the man said that he couldn't answer the question about his father's cause of death.

The salesman wanted to know why. After some embarrassment the client explained that his father had been hanged.

The salesman pondered for a moment. "Just write, 'Father was taking part in a public function when the platform gave way.'"

Hans Schmidt

A man was walking down the street and noticed a sign reading, "Hans Schmidt's Chinese Laundry." Being of a curious nature, he entered and was greeted by an obviously Asian man who identified himself as Hans Schmidt.

"How do you happen to have a name like that?" inquired the stranger.

The Asian man explained in very broken English that when he landed in America, he was standing in the immigration line behind a German. When asked his name, the German replied, "Hans Schmidt." When the immigration official asked the Asian man his name, he replied, "Sam Ting."

Happy

Husband: Now, that looks like a happily married couple.

Wife: Don't be too sure, my dear. They're probably saying the same thing about us.

Harsh

Husband: Now look, Lucy. I don't want to seem harsh, but your mother has been living with us for twenty years now. Don't you think it's about time she got a place of her own?

Wife: *My* mother? I thought she was *your* mother!

Hatchet

There's no point in burying a hatchet if you're going to put up a marker on the site.

Hay

One Sunday as a farmer was getting in his hay crop, his minister stopped by. The pastor asked the farmer if he had been to church. "To tell the truth, I would rather sit on the hay load and think about church than sit in the church and think about hay."

Heaven

A new group of male applicants had just arrived in heaven.

Peter looked them over and said, "All men who were henpecked on earth, please step to the left; all those who were bosses in their own homes, step to the right."

The line quickly formed on the left. Only one man stepped to the right.

Peter looked at the frail little man standing by himself and inquired, "What makes you think you belong on that side?"

Without hesitation, the meek little man explained, "This is where my wife told me to stand."

Heir

Stranger: Good morning, Doctor. I just dropped in to tell you how much I benefited from your treatment.

Doctor: But you're not one of my patients.

Stranger: I know. But my Uncle Bill was, and I'm his heir.

Hiccups

A man rushed into a drugstore and asked a pharmacist for something to stop hiccups. The druggist poured a glass of water and threw it into the man's face.

"Why did you do that?" the man exploded angrily.

"Well, you don't have hiccups now, do you?"

"No!" shouted the customer. "But my wife out in the car still does!"

Historical

"But, Pastor," lamented the young husband in counseling, "whenever Joan and I quarrel, she becomes historical."

"You mean, hysterical?"

"No, historical. She is always digging up my past."

Ho! Ho! Ho!

A man returned to his sports car to find a freshly crushed fender and this note affixed to his windshield wiper: "The people who saw me sideswipe your fender are now watching me write this note, and they doubtless think I'm telling you my name and address so you can contact me and send me the bill. Ho! Ho! Ho! You should live so long."

Hog Caller

A local pastor joined a community service club, and the members thought they would have some fun with him. Under his name on the badge they printed "Hog Caller" as his occupation.

Everyone made a big fanfare as the badge was presented. The pastor responded by saying: "I usually am called the Shepherd of the Sheep, but you know your people better than I do."

Horse Sense

Q. What is another name for stable thinking?
A. Horse sense.

Horseradish

A minister who was very fond of pure, hot horseradish always kept a bottle of it on his dining room table. He offered some to a guest, who took a big spoonful.

When the guest was finally able to speak, he gasped, "I've heard many ministers preach hellfire, but you're the first one I've met who offered a sample."

Hours

Applicant: Before I take this job, tell me—are the hours long?

Employer: No, only sixty minutes each.

Hudson River

A boastful Britisher was bragging about his watch to friends in New York City. At last one of the Americans decided he could stand it no longer.

"That's nothing," he interrupted. "I dropped my watch into the Hudson a year ago, and it's been running ever since."

The Englishman looked taken aback. "What?" he exclaimed. "The same watch?"

"No," he replied, "the Hudson."

Hunter

First hunter: How do you know you hit that duck?

Second hunter: Because I shot him in the foot and in the head at the same time.

First hunter: How could you possibly hit him in the foot and head at the same time?

Second hunter: He was scratching his head.

I Don't Get It

Wife to husband: "Look, Ralph, the first garden tools are peeping their heads above the snow."

I Mean

It's not always easy to say the right thing on the spur of the moment. We can sympathize with the man who met an old friend after many years.

"How is your wife?"

"She is in heaven," replied the friend.

"Oh, I'm sorry," stammered the man. Then he realized this was not the thing to say. "I mean," he stammered, "I'm glad." That seemed even worse so he blurted, "Well, what I really mean is, 'I'm surprised.'"

I'm For It

A parishioner dozed off to sleep during the morning service.

"Will all who want to go to heaven stand?" the preacher asked. All stood except the sleeping parishioner.

After they sat down, the pastor continued, "Well, will all who want to go to the other place stand?"

Somebody suddenly dropped a songbook, and the sleeping man jumped to his feet and stood sheepishly facing the preacher. He mumbled, "Well, Preacher, I don't know what we're voting for, but it looks like you and I are the only ones for it."

I'm Impressed

An Air Force major was promoted to colonel and received a brand-new office. His first morning behind the desk, an airman knocked on the door and asked to speak to him. The colonel, feeling the urge to impress the young airman, picked up his phone.

"Yes, General, thank you. Yes I will pass that along to the president this afternoon. Yes, goodbye, sir."

Then turning to the airman, he barked, "And what do you want?"

"Nothing important, sir," said the airman. "I just came to install your telephone."

I'm Sick of This

Nobody is sicker than the man who is sick on his day off.

Idea

Ben: I've got an idea.
Jen: Be kind to it. It's a long way from home.

Ideas

Ideas die quickly in some people's heads because they can't stand solitary confinement.

Imaginary

Teacher: What is the axis of the earth?
Student: The axis of the earth is an imaginary line that passes from one pole to the other and on which the earth revolves.
Teacher: Very good. Now, could you hang clothes on that line?
Student: Yes, sir.

Teacher: Really? What sort of clothes?

Student: Imaginary clothes, sir.

Improve

Of all the awkward people in your house, there is only one you can improve very much.

Income Tax

Did you hear about the man from the IRS who phoned a certain Baptist minister to say, "We're checking the tax return of a member of your church, Deacon Smith, and notice he lists a donation to your building fund of three hundred dollars. Is that correct?"

The minister answered without hesitation, "I haven't got my records available, but I'll promise you one thing—if he hasn't, he will!"

■ ■ ■

Don't be surprised if your next income-tax form is simplified to contain only four lines:

1. What was your income last year?

2. What were your expenses?

3. How much do you have left?

4. Send it in.

Inflation

Son: Dad, what is "creeping inflation"?

Father: It's when your mother goes shopping for new shoes and ends up with a complete new outfit.

Ingratitude

My brother was sort of odd. I remember once on his birthday, he fell down a dry well, so we lowered his birthday cake to him. He didn't even tug on the rope to say thanks.

Insecure

Mother of small boy to child psychiatrist: "Well, I don't know whether he feels insecure, but everybody else in the neighborhood certainly does!"

Insurance

Jack: Don't you know that you can't sell insurance without a license?

Buck: I knew I wasn't selling any, but I didn't know the reason.

■ ■ ■

The following quotations were taken from a Toronto newspaper. They are samples of comments that individuals wrote down on their claim forms following their auto accidents.

- I misjudged a lady crossing the street.
- Coming home, I drove into the wrong house and collided with a tree I don't have.

- The other car collided with mine without giving warning of its intentions.

- I heard a horn blow and was struck in the back—a lady was evidently trying to pass me.

- I thought my window was down, but found it was up when I put my hand through it.

- My car was stolen and sent up a human cry, but it has not been recovered.

- I collided with a stationary truck coming the other way.

- The truck backed through my windshield into my wife's face.

- A pedestrian hit me and went under my car.

- The guy was all over the road. I had to swerve a number of times before I hit him.

- If the other driver had stopped a few yards behind himself, the accident would not have happened.

- In my attempt to kill a fly, I drove into a telephone pole.

- I had been shopping for plants all day and was on my way home. As I reached an intersection, a hedge sprang up, obscuring my vision. I did not see the other car.

- I had been driving my car for 40 years

when I fell asleep at the wheel and had an accident.

- I was on my way to the doctor's with rear-end trouble when my universal joint gave way, causing me to have an accident.

- My car was legally parked as it backed into the other vehicle.

- An invisible car came out of nowhere, struck my vehicle, and vanished.

- I told the police that I was not injured, but on removing my hat, I found that I had a skull fracture.

- I was sure the old fellow would never make it to the other side of the roadway when I struck him.

- The pedestrian had no idea which way to go, so I ran over him.

- The indirect cause of this accident was a little guy in a small car with a big mouth.

- I was thrown from my car as it left the road. I was later found in a ditch by some stray cows.

- The telephone pole was approaching fast. I was attempting to swerve out of its path when it struck my front end.

- I was unable to stop in time, and my car crashed into the other vehicle. The driver

and passengers then left immediately for a
vacation with injuries.

* I pulled away from the side of the road,
  glanced at my mother-in-law, and headed
  over the embankment.

Intelligence

Two men were digging a ditch on a very hot day.
One said to the other, "Why are we down in this hole
digging a ditch when our boss is standing up there in
the shade of a tree?"

"I don't know," responded the other. "I'll ask him."
So he climbed out of the hole and went to his boss.
"Why are we digging in the hot sun and you are stand-
ing in the shade?"

"Intelligence," the boss said.

"What do you mean, 'intelligence'?"

The boss said, "Well, I'll show you. I'll put my hand
on this tree, and I want you to hit it with your fist as
hard as you can." The ditchdigger took a mighty swing
and tried to hit the boss's hand. The boss removed his
hand, and the ditchdigger hit the tree. The boss said,
"That's intelligence!"

The ditchdigger went back to his hole. His friend
asked, "What did he say?"

"He said we are down here because of intelligence."

"What's intelligence?" said the friend.

The ditchdigger put his hand on his face and said,
"Take your shovel and hit my hand."

Interrupt

Member to pastor at the end of the morning service: "Pastor, you were really good this morning! You interrupted my thoughts at least half a dozen times!"

Introduction

Tonight I would like to present to you _____, of whom the president of the United States once said: "Who?"

■ ■ ■

It is said that _____ is the greatest speaker in the business. And tonight we honor the man who made that statement, _____.

Inventor

Did you hear about the inventor who came up with a knife that would slice two loaves of bread at the same time? He sold it to a large bakery. He then developed a knife that could slice three loaves of bread at the same time. He sold that idea too.

Finally, the ultimate. He made a huge knife that could cut four loaves of bread at the same time! And so was born the world's first four-loaf cleaver.

IQ

He had an extremely high IQ when he was five. Too bad he grew out of it.

IRS

April is always a difficult month for Americans. Even if your ship comes in, the IRS is right there to help you unload it.

■ ■

IRS agent to taxpayer: "I'm afraid we can't allow you to deduct last year's tax as a bad investment."

■ ■

Ted: What kind of work do you do?
Fred: I work for the IRS.
Ted: Doesn't everybody?

■ ■

A businessman who was near death asked that his remains be cremated and the ashes be mailed to the Internal Revenue Service with the following note attached: "Now you have it all."

It's Flooded

Wife: Honey, I can't get the car started. I think it's flooded.
Husband: Where is it?
Wife: In the swimming pool.

It's His Problem

Wife: George! Come quickly! A wild tiger has just gone into mother's tent!

Husband: Well, he got himself into that mess; he can get himself out of it!

It's the Plumber

Once upon a time there was a parrot who could say only three little words: "Who is it?" One day when the parrot was alone in the house, there was a loud knock on the door. "Who is it?" screeched the parrot.

"It's the plumber," the visitor responded.

"Who is it?" repeated the parrot.

"It's the plumber, I tell you," was the reply. "You called me to tell me your cellar was flooded."

Again the parrot called, "Who is it?"

By this time, the plumber became so angry that he fainted. A neighbor rushed over to see the cause of the commotion, and found that the visitor had died because of a heart attack. The neighbor looked at the man and said, "Who is it?"

The parrot answered, "It's the plumber!"

Job

Father: My son just received his BA.
Neighbor: I suppose now he'll be looking for a PhD.
Father: No, now he's looking for a J-O-B.

John Smith

John Smith happened to witness a minor holdup. In due time the police arrived, and one officer asked the witness his name.

"John Smith," said Smith.

"Cut the comedy," snapped the cop. "What's your real name?"

"All right," said Smith, "put me down as Winston Churchill."

"That's more like it," said the officer. "You can't fool me with that Smith stuff."

Judge

A lady was showing a church friend her neighbor's wash through her back window. "Our neighbor isn't very clean. Look at those streaks on the wash!"

Replied her friend, "Those streaks aren't on your neighbor's wash. They're on your window."

Julius Caesar

Psychiatrist: Congratulations, sir, you're cured.

Patient: Some cure. When I started therapy, I was Julius Caesar. Now I'm nobody.

Karate

Wife: You both arrived at that cab at the same time. Why did you let him have it? Why didn't you stand up for your rights?

Husband: He needed it more than I did. He was late to his karate class.

Kayak

Two Eskimos sitting in a kayak were chilly, but when they lit a fire in the craft it sank—proving once and for all that you can't have your kayak and heat it too.

Kibitzer

All evening long four cardplayers had been pestered by a kibitzer. When he went out of the room for a moment, they hit on a plan to silence him. "Let's make up a game no one ever heard of," one of them said. "Then he'll have to shut up."

The kibitzer returned. The dealer tore two cards in half and gave them to the man on his left. He tore the corners off three cards and spread them out in front of the man opposite him. Then he tore five cards in quarters, gave fifteen pieces to the man on his right and kept five himself. "I have a mingle," he said. "I'll bet a dollar."

"I have a snazzle," the next man announced. "I'll raise you a dollar."

The third man folded without betting. The fourth, after due deliberation, said, "I've got a farfle. I'll raise you two dollars."

The kibitzer shook his head vehemently. "You're crazy," he said. "You're never going to beat a mingle and a snazzle with a lousy farfle!"

Kick in the Pants

Dad: How dare you kick your little brother in the stomach!

Son: It's his own fault, Daddy. He turned around.

Kids

Children would all be brought up perfectly if families would just swap kids. Everyone knows what ought to be done with the neighbor's kids.

■ ■ ■

One nice thing about kids is that they don't keep telling you boring stories about the clever things their parents said.

King

A lion was walking through the jungle taking a poll to determine who was the greatest among all the wild animals. When he saw the hippopotamus, he inquired, "Who is king of the jungle?"

"You are," said the hippopotamus.

Next he met a giraffe. "Who is king of the jungle?" he inquired.

"You are," said the giraffe.

Then he met a tiger and said, "Who is king of the jungle?"

"Oh, you are," said the tiger.

Finally he met an elephant. He gave him a good rap on the knee and said, "And who is king of the jungle?"

The elephant picked him up in his trunk and swung him against a large tree. As the lion bounced off the tree and hit the ground, he got up and dusted himself off and said, "You don't have to get so mad just because you don't know the right answer."

King Herod

A seminary class addressed the problem of King Herod offering up half his kingdom to see the daughter of Herodias dance.

"Now, what if you offered her anything she wanted, and the girl asked for the head of John the Baptist. You don't want to murder John, so what would you do?" asked the professor.

Soon a hand was raised. "I'd tell her that the head of John the Baptist was in the other half."

Kipper

For many years a certain white whale and a tiny herring had been inseparable friends. Wherever the white whale roamed in search of food, the herring was sure to be swimming right along beside him.

One fine spring day the herring turned up off the coast of Norway without his companion. Naturally all the other fish were curious, and an octopus finally asked the herring what happened to his whale friend.

"How should I know?" the herring replied. "Am I my blubber's kipper?"

Kiss

He: I promise you, the next time you contradict me, I'm going to kiss you.

She: Oh no you're not!

■ ■ ■

Bill: Am I the only man you have ever kissed?
Sue: Yes, and by far the best looking.

* * *

Stealing a kiss may be petty larceny, but sometimes it's grand.

* * *

A kiss is a peculiar proposition—of no use to one, yet absolute bliss to two. The small boy gets it for nothing, the young man has to lie for it, and the old man has to buy it. It is the baby's right, the lover's privilege, and the hypocrite's mask. To a young girl, it shows faith; to a married woman, hope; and to an elderly widow, charity.

Knitting

Son: Why do the ladies always bring their knitting when they come to visit?

Father: So they will have something to think about while they talk.

Language

Q. What's more clever than speaking in several languages?

A. Keeping your mouth shut in one.

Large Red Cow

A man's car stalled on a country road. When he got out to fix it, a cow came along and stopped beside him. "Your trouble is probably in the carburetor," said the cow.

Startled, the man jumped back and ran down the road until he met a farmer. He told the farmer his story.

"Was it a large red cow with a brown spot over the right eye?" asked the farmer.

"Yes, yes," the man replied.

"Oh! I wouldn't listen to Bessie," said the farmer. "She doesn't know anything about cars."

Last Resort

I just heard of a man who met his wife at a travel bureau. She was looking for a vacation, and he was the last resort.

The Last Straw

Guest: What on earth do you put in your mattresses?

Innkeeper: The finest straw, sir.

Guest: Now I know where the straw that broke the camel's back came from.

Late to Work

Every day Mr. Smith's secretary was 20 minutes late to work. Then one day she slid snugly into place only five minutes tardy.

"Well," said Mr. Smith, "This is the earliest you've ever been late."

Lawn Mower

Wife: I'm happy to see that the neighbors finally returned our lawn mower before they moved. They certainly had it long enough.

Husband: *Our* lawn mower? I just bought it at their garage sale!

Lawyer

A lawyer was approached by his friend, a priest, who wanted a will drawn up. When the work was completed and ready to be mailed, the lawyer couldn't resist inserting this note: "Thy will be done."

Leftovers

The lady said to the waitress, "May I have a bag to carry leftovers to my dog?"

Her six-year-old said, "Oh Mother, are we going to get a dog?"

Let Me Out

At a lecture series a very poor speaker was on the platform. As he was speaking, people in the audience began to get up and leave. After about ten minutes there was only one man left. Finally the man stopped speaking and asked the man why he remained to the end.

"I'm the next speaker."

Let's Make a Deal

A farmer and his wife went to a fair. The farmer was fascinated by the airplane rides, but he balked at the $20 tickets.

"Let's make a deal," said the pilot. "If you and your wife can ride without making a single sound, I won't charge you anything. Otherwise you each pay the twenty dollars."

"Good deal!" said the farmer.

So they went for a ride. When they got back the pilot said, "If I hadn't been there, I never would have believed it. You never made a sound!"

"It wasn't easy," said the farmer. "I almost yelled when my wife fell out."

Letter

Suddenly called out of town, a news commentator told his new secretary, "Write Allis-Chalmers in Milwaukee. Say that I can't keep that appointment Friday. I'm off for Texas. I'll telephone when I get back. Sign my name."

Upon his return, he found this copy on his desk:

Alice Chalmers
Milwaukee, Wisconsin

Dear Alice,
I'm off for Texas and can't keep that date...

The man promptly phoned the company and said, "I hope you haven't received a certain letter."

"Received it!" came the reply. "It's been on the bulletin board for three days!"

■ ■ ■

Letter from son at school:

Dear Dad,

Gue$$ what I need mo$t. That'$ right. $end it $oon.

Be$t wi$he$,
Jay

Reply:

Dear Jay,

NOthing ever happens here. We kNOw you like school. Write aNOther letter soon. Mom was asking about you at NOon.

NOw I have to say goodbye.
Dad

Lies

The following will help you to identify common lies:

I'm only thinking of you, dear. *Meaning*: I am now about to get a bit of my own back.

I don't want to make you unhappy. *Meaning*: I will now repeat to you certain malicious gossip which will reduce you to sleepless misery.

I'm bound to admit. *Meaning*: I will now confuse the main issue.

I'm not one to criticize. *Meaning*: I shall now proceed to find fault with all you have done.

I'm as broad-minded as anyone. *Meaning*: All my ideas on this subject are hopelessly out-of-date.

I hope I know my place. *Meaning*: I am about to step right out of it and tell you a few home truths.

I'm a tolerant sort of fellow. *Meaning*: I can't endure you for another moment and am now preparing to throw you out of the house.

Life Jackets

An ocean liner was sinking, and the captain yelled, "Does anybody know how to pray?"

A minister on board said, "I do."

"Good," said the captain. "You start praying. The rest of us will put on the life jackets. We are one short."

Like a Frog

Little girl: Grandfather, make like a frog.

Grandfather: What do you mean, make like a frog?

Little girl: Mommy says we're going to make a lot of money when you croak!

Limburger Cheese

Did you hear about the garlic and Limburger cheese diet? You don't lose any weight, but your friends will think you look thinner at a distance.

Linguist

Peg: I hear your husband is a linguist.

Meg: Yes, he speaks three languages—golf, football, and baseball.

Little

A man went to the psychiatrist and complained about feeling inferior because of his height. The psychiatrist reminded him about great men in history who were short, such as Napoleon and Toulouse-Lautrec.

The little man felt completely cured after talking to the psychiatrist, and everything would have worked out fine, but as he went out of the doctor's office a cat ate him.

■ ■ ■

During the days of the Salem, Massachusetts, witch hunts, a little person was imprisoned for fortune-telling. She later escaped from jail, and the headline in the local newspaper read, "Small Medium at Large."

Loafers

During an Army war game, a commanding officer's jeep got stuck in the mud. The CO saw some men lounging nearby and asked them to help him get unstuck.

"Sorry, sir," said one of the loafers, "but we've been classified dead, and the umpire said we couldn't contribute in any way."

The CO turned to his driver. "Go drag a couple of those dead bodies over here and throw them under the wheels to give us some traction."

Loan

John: Lend me fifty.

Jack: I have only forty.

John: Well, let me have the forty and you can owe me the ten.

Long Hair

A long-haired boy was trying to get into a swim club but was stopped by the owner, who tried to explain that for health reasons, long hair was not allowed in the pool.

"Get a swim cap or a haircut, and you're welcome," said the owner.

"Some of history's greatest men had long hair," said the young man.

"Those are the rules."

"Moses had long hair."

"Moses can't swim in our pool either."

Loophole

On visiting a seriously ill lawyer in the hospital, his friend found him sitting up in bed, frantically leafing through the Bible.

"What are you doing?" asked the friend.

"Looking for loopholes," replied the lawyer.

Lord's Prayer

Two lawyers were bosom buddies. Much to the amazement of one, the other became a Sunday school teacher. "I bet you don't even know the Lord's Prayer," the first one said.

"Everybody knows that," the other replied. "It's 'Now I lay me down to sleep...'"

"You win," said the first one. "I didn't know you knew so much about the Bible."

Love

Better to have loved a short man than never to have loved a tall.

■ ■ ■

Love may be blind, but it seems to be able to find its way around in the dark.

■ ■ ■

Girl: Do you love me?
Boy: Yes, dear.
Girl: Would you die for me?
Boy: No—mine is an undying love.

■ ■ ■

Becky: Do you love me with all your heart and soul?
Dave: Uh-huh.
Becky: Do you think I'm the most beautiful girl in the world?

Dave: Uh-huh.
Becky: Do you think my lips are like rose petals?
Dave: Uh-huh.
Becky: Oh, you say the most beautiful things.

■ ■ ■

John: I can't seem to get anywhere with Jan.
Jack: What happened?
John: I told her I was knee-deep in love with her.
Jack: What was her reaction?
John: She promised to put me on her wading list.

Lucky Saucer

In front of a delicatessen, an art connoisseur noticed a mangy little kitten lapping up milk from a saucer. The saucer, he realized with a start, was a rare and precious piece of pottery.

He sauntered into the store and offered two dollars for the cat. "It's not for sale," said the proprietor.

"Look," said the collector, "that cat is dirty and undesirable, but I'm eccentric. I like cats that way. I'll raise my offer to five dollars."

"It's a deal," said the proprietor, and pocketed the five on the spot.

"For that sum I'm sure you won't mind throwing in the saucer," said the connoisseur. "The kitten seems so happy drinking from it."

"Nothing doing," said the proprietor firmly. "That's my lucky saucer. From that saucer, so far this week I've sold thirty-four cats."

Lying

A minister concluded the Sunday service by saying, "Next Sunday I'm going to preach on the subject of liars. In preparation, I would like you all to read the seventeenth chapter of Mark."

On the following Sunday, the preacher rose and said, "Now then, all of you who have read the seventeenth chapter of Mark as I requested, please raise your hands." Nearly every hand in the congregation went up. Then said the preacher, "You are the people I want to talk to. There is no seventeenth chapter of Mark."

Makes Sense to Me

Employer: We can pay you four hundred dollars a week now and five hundred dollars a week in eight months.

Applicant: Thank you. I'll drop back in eight months.

Marbles

In order to become a good speaker, you must go to diction school, where coaches teach you how to speak clearly. To do this, they fill your mouth with marbles, and you're supposed to talk clearly right through the marbles. Every day you lose one marble. When you've lost all your marbles…

Masks

When I got the bill for my operation, I realized why surgeons wear masks in the operating room.

Mathematics

A Missouri farmer passed away and left 17 mules to his three sons. His will said that the oldest boy was to get one-half of the mules, the second eldest one-third, and the youngest one-ninth. The three sons, recognizing the difficulty of dividing 17 mules into these fractions, began to argue.

Their uncle heard about the argument, hitched up his mule, and drove out to settle the matter. He added his mule to the 17, making 18. The eldest son therefore got one-half, or nine; the second got one-third, or six; and the youngest got one-ninth, or two. Adding up 9, 6, and 2 equals 17. The uncle, having settled the argument, hitched up his mule and drove home.

Maxed Out

Max looked up at the steep, icy mountainside. "I can't do it," he said.

His companions begged him to climb the mountain with them, but he refused to move. "I'm against mountain climbing," he said.

Now they call him "Anti-climb Max."

Mayflower

"My ancestors came over on the *Mayflower*."

"Don't feel bad about it. We can't all be born here."

Me Too

A Texas rancher was visiting an Iowa farm. The Iowa farmer was justly proud of his 200 acres of rich, productive land.

"Is this your whole farm?" the Texan asked. "Back in Texas, I get in my car at five in the morning, and I drive and drive all day. At dusk I just reach the end of my ranch."

The Iowa farmer thought a while and replied, "I used to have a car like that too."

Medicine

The doctor told me to take this medicine after a hot bath. I could hardly finish drinking the bath!

Melody in F (The Prodigal Son)

Feeling footloose and frisky, a featherbrained fellow
Forced his fond father to fork over the farthings
And flew far to foreign fields
And frittered his fortune feasting fabulously with faithless friends.
Fleeced by his fellows in folly and facing famine,
He found himself a feed-flinger in a filthy farmyard.
Fairly famishing, he fain would have filled his frame
With foraged food from fodder fragments.
"Phooey, my father's flunkies fare far finer,"
The frazzled fugitive forlornly fumbled, frankly facing facts.
Frustrated by failure and filled with foreboding,
He fled forthwith to his family.

Falling at his father's feet, he forlornly fumbled,
"Father, I've flunked
And fruitlessly forfeited family fellowship favor."
The farsighted father, forestalling further flinching,
Frantically flagged the flunkies to
Fetch a fatling from the flock and fix a feast.
The fugitive's faultfinding brother frowned
On fickle forgiveness of former folderol.
But the faithful father figured,
"Filial fidelity is fine, but the fugitive is found!
What forbids fervent festivity?
Let flags be unfurled! Let fanfares flare!"
Father's forgiveness formed the foundation
For the former fugitive's future fortitude!

Memory Loss

There are three ways to tell if you are getting old: first, a loss of memory. Second…

Mental Block

A mental block is a street on which several psychiatrists live.

Mental Patients

When a busload of people entered a large restaurant, the leader of the group approached the manager.

"Sir, I'm Mr. Phillips of the Kingsview Mental Hospital. These nice folks are patients in our halfway-house program. They've all been cured, but they do have one small problem—they will want to pay you in bottle caps. So if you'll be so kind as to humor them in this way, I'll take care of the bill when they are through."

The manager, wanting to be a good citizen, collected the bottle caps. The leader returned and with gratitude said, "Thank you so very much. I'll pay the bill now. Do you have change for a hubcap?"

Mentally Ill

One out of four Americans is mentally ill. Next time you're in a group of four people, take a good look at the other three. If they look all right, you're it!

Metal Age

We live in the Metal Age:
silver in the hair,
gold in the teeth,
iron in the veins, and
lead in the pants.

Middle Age

Middle age is when you know all the answers but nobody asks you the questions.

Millionaire

A millionaire is a billionaire after taxes.

Mind

Jay: I have half a mind to get married.
Bob: That's all you need.

Minister

The new minister stood at the church door, greeting the members as they left the Sunday morning service. Most of the people graciously told the new minister how they liked his message. But one man said, "That was a very dull and boring sermon, Pastor."

In a few minutes the same man appeared again in line and said, "I don't think you did any preparation for your message, Pastor."

Once again, the man appeared, this time muttering, "You really blew it. You didn't have a thing to say, Pastor."

Finally the minister could stand it no longer. He went over to one of the deacons and inquired about the man.

"Oh, don't let that guy bother you," said the deacon. "He is a little slow. All he does is go around repeating whatever he hears other people saying."

■ ■ ■

A minister was asked to inform a man with a heart condition that he had just inherited a million dollars. Everyone was afraid the shock would cause a heart attack and the man would die.

The minister went to the man's house and said, "Joe, what would you do if you inherited a million dollars?"

Joe responded, "Well, Pastor, I think I would give half of it to the church."

The minister fell over dead.

Minor Operation

A minor operation is one performed on somebody else.

Miserable

Bev: You know, girls, a lot of men are going to be miserable when I marry.

Dev: Really? How many men are you going to marry?

Money Talk

Money talks—it says goodbye.

Moody

My husband has three moods: hungry, thirsty, and both.

Morning

If the Lord wanted us to enjoy sunrises, they would come at ten in the morning.

Moses

Teacher: If Moses were alive today, he'd be considered a remarkable man.

Lenny: He ought to be—he'd be more than twenty-five hundred years old.

Mother's Day

Mother's Day brings back memories of maternal advice and admonition. Picture the scene with these famous offspring:

Alexander the Great's mother: "How many times do I have to tell you—you can't have everything you want in this world!"

Franz Schubert's mother: "Take my advice, son. Never start anything you can't finish."

Achilles's mother: "Stop imagining things. There's nothing wrong with your heel."

Madame de Pompadour's mother: "For heaven's sake, child, do something about your hair!"

Sigmund Freud's mother: "Stop pestering me! I've told you a hundred times the stork brought you!"

Motivation

A young man had a job with a company that required him to work very late at night. In going home after work, he found that it was fastest to walk through a cemetery near his home. One night when he was very tired, he accidentally fell into a freshly dug grave.

At first he was not too concerned, but when he realized that he could not get out because the hole was too deep, he became somewhat hysterical. Finally, in complete exhaustion, he sat down in the corner of the grave and fell asleep.

Shortly thereafter another man decided to walk through the cemetery and happened to fall into the same grave. He too went through great effort to get out but could not. He then moved around the grave until he stepped on the first man who was asleep. The first man woke up and shouted, "You can't get out of here!"

But the second man did.

Motorcycle

Two men were traveling on a motorcycle on a windy winter day. When it became too breezy for the passenger, they stopped so he could put his overcoat on backward to keep the wind from ballooning it away from him.

A few miles further on, the motorcycle hit a tree, killing the driver and stunning the fellow with the reversed coat. Later, when the coroner visited the scene, he asked a rookie policeman standing nearby, "What happened?"

"Well," the officer replied, "one of them was dead when I got here, and by the time I got the head of the other one straightened around, he was dead too."

Mountains

Rob: I climb mountains because they are there.

Bob: That's the reason everybody else goes around them!

Mouse

Teacher: Robert Burns wrote "To a Mouse."

Student: I'll bet he didn't get an answer.

Mousetrap

Young wife: Don't forget to bring home another mousetrap.

Husband: What's the matter with the one I brought yesterday?

Young wife: It's full!

Mouth First

He is the only person who enters the room mouth first!

Mozart

A married couple trying to live up to a snobbish lifestyle went to a party. The conversation turned to Mozart. "Absolutely brilliant, magnificent, a genius!"

The woman, wanting to join in the conversation, remarked casually, "Ah, Mozart. You're so right. I love him. Only this morning I saw him getting on the number five bus going to Coney Island." There was a sudden hush, and everyone looked at her. Her husband was mortified. He pulled her away and whispered, "We're leaving right now. Get your coat and let's get out of here."

As they drove home, he kept muttering to himself. Finally his wife turned to him. "You're angry about something."

"Oh really? You noticed?" he sneered. "I've never been so embarrassed in my life! You saw Mozart take the number five bus to Coney Island? You idiot! Don't you know the number five bus doesn't go to Coney Island?"

Mud Hole

A motorist, after being bogged down in a muddy road, paid a passing farmer $20 to pull him out with his tractor. After he was back on dry ground he said to the farmer, "At that price, I should think you would be pulling people out of the mud night and day."

"Can't," replied the farmer. "At night I haul water for the hole."

Mud Pack

Bill: Every once in a while my wife puts on one of those mud packs.

Will: Does it improve her looks?

Bill: Only for a few days. Then the mud falls off.

Mud Pies

A man pleaded with the psychiatrist, "You've got to help me. It's my son."

"What's the matter?"

"He's always eating mud pies. I get up in the morning, and there he is in the backyard, eating mud pies. I come home at lunch, and he is eating mud pies. I come home at dinner, and there he is in the backyard, eating mud pies."

The psychiatrist reassured him, "Give the kid a chance. It's all part of growing up. It'll pass."

"Well, I don't like it, and neither does his wife."

Murder

"Have you ever thought about divorcing your wife?"
"Divorce? No. Murder? Yes."

My First

"Excuse me for being nervous," the sheriff apologized as he slipped the noose over the condemned man's head. "This is my first hanging."

"Mine too!" the condemned man replied.

My Lucky Number

Thirteen ministers were on a flight to New York. When they came into a large storm, they told the stewardess to tell the pilot that everything would be okay because 13 ministers were on board.

Later the stewardess returned from the cockpit.

"What did the pilot say?" one preacher asked.

"He said he was glad to have thirteen ministers aboard, but he would rather have four good engines."

Nearsighted

Jack: I'm so nearsighted I nearly worked myself to death.

Elmer: What's being nearsighted got to do with working yourself to death?

Jack: I couldn't tell whether the boss was watching me or not, so I had to work all the time.

Neighbors

The only people who listen to both sides of an argument are the neighbors.

Night

Late-staying guest: Well, goodnight. I hope I haven't kept you up too late.

Yawning host: Not at all. We would have been getting up soon anyway.

Nobody Likes Me

The mother was having a hard time getting her son to go to school in the morning.

"Nobody in school likes me," he complained. "The teachers don't like me, the kids don't like me, the superintendent wants to transfer me, the bus drivers hate me, the school board wants me to drop out, and the custodians have it in for me. I don't want to go to school."

"But you have to go to school," countered his mother. "You're healthy, you have a lot to learn, you have something to offer others, and you're a leader. Besides, you're forty-five years old, and you're the principal."

Nonconformist

A man entered a barbershop and said, "I'm tired of looking like everyone else. I want a change—part my hair from ear to ear!"

"Are you sure?"

"Yes," said the man.

The barber did as he was told, and a satisfied customer left the shop.

Three hours passed and the man reentered the shop. "Put it back the way it was," he said.

"What's the matter?" said the barber. "Are you tired of being a nonconformist already?"

"No," he replied. "I'm tired of people whispering in my nose!"

Not Bad

"How long have you two been married?" asked a friend.

"We've been happily married for seven years," answered the husband. "Seven out of sixteen isn't bad."

Not Here

Joe and Bill met on a street corner. When Joe said he was glad to see his friend, Bill answered, "How can you see me when I'm not even here? And I'll bet you ten dollars I can prove it!"

"You're going to bet me ten dollars you're not here? Okay, it's a bet. Go ahead and prove it."

"Am I in Chicago?"

"Nope."

"Am I in New York?"

"No!"

"Well, if I'm not in Chicago and I'm not in New York, that means I'm in some other place, right?"

"That's right."

Bill said, "Well, if I'm in some other place, I can't be here. I'll take that ten dollars."

Joe replied, "How can I give you the money if you're not here?"

Note

The following note was fastened to a defective parking meter with a rubber band:

"I put three nickels in this meter. License number 4761PQ."

"FRD719—me too!"

"So did I—JRY335."

"I'm not going to pay a nickel to find out if these guys are lying. WTM259."

Notes

A minister preached a very short sermon. He explained, "My dog got into my office and chewed up some of my notes."

At the close of the service a visitor asked, "If your dog ever has pups, may my pastor have one?"

Nothing

Most of us know how to say nothing, but few of us know when.

Nothing's Wrong

The airline company was disturbed over a high number of accidents and decided to eliminate human errors by building a completely mechanical plane.

"Ladies and gentlemen," came a voice over a loudspeaker on the maiden flight, "it may interest you to know that you are now traveling in the world's first completely automatic plane. Now just sit back and relax because nothing can possibly go wrong...go wrong... go wrong...go wrong..."

Nudity

Phyllis Diller once said there was so much nudity in films that an Oscar for costume design would one day go to a dermatologist.

Numbers

If we switch to the metric system, we may have to say...

- A miss is as good as 1.6 kilometers.
- Put your best 0.3 of a meter forward.
- Spare the 5.03 meters and spoil the child.
- Twenty-eight grams of prevention is worth 453 grams of cure.
- Give a man 2.5 centimeters and he'll take 1.6 kilometers.
- Peter Piper picked 8.8 liters of pickled peppers.

Nuts to You

A pastor and his wife received this note with a box of goodies from a parishioner:

"Dear Pastor, knowing that you do not eat sweets, I am sending candy to your wife and nuts to you."

Off and Running

Two men went to the train station with a friend. The train was late, so they sat down for a cup of coffee. They talked and sipped their coffee and forgot all about the train. Suddenly they heard the last announcement about the departing train, so they all got up and started running. When they reached the train, it was just pulling out of the station, so they started running down the tracks. Two of the men just made it to the last car, but the third man was not quite fast enough. He slowed to a stop and started laughing. An onlooker saw him and asked, "What are you laughing for? You just missed your train."

"You're right," was the reply. "I did miss my train. What's funny is that those two men came to see me off."

Offering

An usher was passing the collection plate at a large church wedding. A guest looked up, very puzzled. Without waiting for the question, the usher nodded his head and said, "I know it's unusual, but the father of the bride requested it."

Oh, Boy

"This house," said the real-estate salesman, "has its good points and its bad points. To show you I'm honest, I'm going to tell you about both. The disadvantages are that there is a chemical plant a block south and a slaughterhouse a block north."

"What are the advantages?" inquired the prospective buyer.

"You can always tell which way the wind is blowing."

Oh, My Aching Back

As a couple left an auditorium after a two-hour lecture on nineteenth-century English poets, the wife exclaimed, "Didn't it make your mind soar?"

"Yes," her husband agreed grimly. "And my backside too."

Okay

A little boy never said a word for six years. One day his parents served him cocoa. From out of nowhere, the kid said, "This cocoa is no good."

His parents were ecstatic. They asked him, "Why did you wait so long to talk?"

He said, "Until now, everything's been okay."

Old Bore

A tired minister was at home resting, and through the window he saw a woman approaching his door. She was one of those too-talkative people, and he was not anxious to talk with her. He said to his wife, "I'll just duck upstairs and wait until she goes away."

An hour passed, so he tiptoed to the stair landing and listened—not a sound. He was very pleased, so he started down calling loudly to his wife, "Well, my dear, did you get rid of that old bore at last?"

The next moment he heard the voice of the same woman caller, and she couldn't possibly have missed hearing him. Two steps down, he saw them both staring up at him. It seemed truly a crisis moment.

The quick-thinking minister's wife answered, "Yes, dear, she went away over an hour ago. But Mrs. Jones has come to call in the meantime, and I'm sure you'll be glad to greet her."

Old Nature

A man was taken to court for stealing an item from a store. The man said to the judge, "Your Honor, I'm a Christian. I've become a new man. But I have an old nature also. It was not my new man who did wrong. It was my old man."

The judge responded, "Since it was the old man that broke the law, we'll sentence him to sixty days in jail. And since the new man was an accomplice in the theft, we'll give him thirty days too. I therefore sentence you both to ninety days in jail."

Older

You can tell you're getting older when…

- You sit in a rocking chair and can't get it going.
- You burn the midnight oil after eight p.m.
- You look forward to a dull evening.
- Your knees buckle but your belt won't.
- Your little black book contains only names ending in MD.
- You decide to procrastinate and never get around to it.
- You walk with your head held high, trying to get used to your bifocals.
- You sink your teeth into a steak and they stay there.

Oops

Customer: I'm sorry, waiter, but I only have enough money for the bill. I have nothing left for a tip.

Waiter: Let me add up that bill again, sir.

Operation

Q. What's the greatest surgical operation on record?

A. Lancing Michigan.

Opportunity

The trouble with opportunity is that it's always more recognizable going than coming.

Optimist

The optimist fell from the top story of a skyscraper. As he passed the tenth story, he was overheard muttering, "So far, so good!"

Pain in the Neck

The man who thinks he knows it all is a pain in the neck to those of us who really do.

■ ■ ■

Teri: How is the pain in your neck?
Shari: He's out playing golf.

Pancakes

The little lady sat quietly in the psychiatrist's office. The good doctor questioned her gently as to why her family wanted her locked up.

"Now, tell me," he said, "just what your trouble is."

"It's just that…just that I'm so fond of pancakes, Doctor."

"Is that all? Why, I'm very fond of pancakes myself."

"Oh Doctor, really? You must come over to our house. I've got trunks and trunks full of them!"

Parachute Jump

Just before a new recruit made his first parachute jump, his sergeant reminded him, "Count to ten and pull the first rip cord. If it snarls, pull the second rip cord for the auxiliary chute. After you land, our truck will pick you up."

The paratrooper took a deep breath and jumped. He counted to ten and pulled the first cord. Nothing happened. He pulled the second cord. Again, nothing happened. As he careened crazily earthward, he said to himself, "Now I'll bet that truck won't be there either!"

Parents

I've wanted to run away from home more often since I've had kids than when I was one.

Pastor

An elderly woman was weeping as she bade good-bye to the man who had been pastor of her church for several years.

"My dear lady," consoled the departing pastor, "don't get so upset. The bishop surely will send a much better pastor to replace me here."

"That's what they told us the last time," wailed the woman.

Pearls

Interrupted by the sound of the bell announcing the end of the class, the professor was annoyed to see his students noisily preparing to leave even though he was in the middle of his lecture. "Just a moment, gentlemen," he said, "I have a few more pearls to cast."

Pelican

A man walked into a doctor's office with a pelican on his head.

"You need help immediately," said the doctor.

"I certainly do," said the pelican. "Get this man out from under me."

Penny-Pincher

A passenger was arguing with a conductor as to whether the fare was $10 or $15. Finally the disgusted conductor picked up the passenger's suitcase and tossed it off the train, just as they passed over a bridge. The suitcase landed with a splash.

The passenger screamed, "Isn't it enough to try to overcharge me? Now you try to drown my little boy!"

Perfect Age

My children are at the perfect age...too old to cry at night and too young to borrow my car.

Perfume

Anyone who thinks chemical warfare is something new doesn't know much about women's perfume.

Personal Check

An old miser, because of his exceptional thrift, had no friends. Just before he died, he called his doctor, lawyer, and minister together around his bedside. "I have always heard you can't take it with you, but I'm going to prove you can," he said. "I have ninety thousand dollars in cash under my mattress. It's in three envelopes of thirty thousand each. I want each of you to take one envelope now, and just before they throw the dirt on me, you throw the envelopes in."

The three attended the funeral, and each threw his envelope into the grave. On the way back from the cemetery, the minister said, "I don't feel exactly right. I'm going to confess—I needed ten thousand badly for a new church we are building, so I took out ten thousand and threw only twenty thousand in the grave."

The doctor said, "I too must confess. I am building a hospital and took twenty thousand. I threw in only ten thousand."

The lawyer said, "Gentlemen, I'm surprised, shocked, and ashamed of you. I don't see how you could hold out that money. I threw in my personal check for the full amount."

Pessimist

A pessimist remembers the lily belongs to the onion family; an optimist counters that the onion belongs to the lily family.

Pinch

A man and his little girl were on an overcrowded elevator. Suddenly a lady in front turned around, slapped the man, and left in a huff.

The little girl remarked, "I didn't like her either, Daddy. She stepped on my toe, so I pinched her."

■ ■ ■

As the crowded elevator descended, Mrs. Wilson became increasingly furious with her husband, who was delighted to be pressed against a gorgeous blonde.

As the elevator stopped at the main floor, the blonde suddenly whirled, slapped Mr. Wilson, and said, "That will teach you to pinch!"

Bewildered, Mr. Wilson was halfway to the parking lot with his wife when he choked, "I…I…didn't pinch that girl."

"Of course you didn't," said his wife. "I did."

Play It by Ear

A man walking along the road saw a cowboy lying with his ear to the ground. He went over and listened. The cowboy said, "Large wheels, green Ford pickup, male driver with large dog next to him, Colorado license plate, traveling about seventy-five miles an hour."

The man was astounded. "You mean you can tell all that just by listening with your ear to the ground?"

"Ear to the ground, nothing," said the cowboy. "That truck just ran over me."

Poise

Q. What is the definition of poise?

A. The ability to keep talking while the other guy takes the check.

Poisoned Coffee

The district attorney was cross-examining the murderer.

"And as your husband sat at the breakfast table drinking the coffee you had poisoned, didn't you feel any qualms? Didn't you feel the slightest pity for him, knowing he was about to die and was wholly unaware of it?"

"Yes, there was a moment when I sort of felt sorry for him."

"When was that?"

"When he asked for the second cup."

Politics

Governmental machinery is the marvelous device that enables ten men to do the work of one.

■ ■ ■

A lobbyist browsing through an encyclopedia came upon a stunning idea. In ancient Greece, in order to prevent statesmen from passing unreasonable laws, lawmakers were asked to introduce all new laws while standing on a platform with a rope around their neck. If the law passed, the rope was removed. If it failed, the platform was removed.

Pontius Pilot

A Sunday school teacher asked her students to draw a picture of the holy family. After the pictures were brought to her, she saw that some of the youngsters had drawn the conventional pictures—the holy family and the manger, Mary riding on the mule, and so on.

But she called up one little boy to ask him to explain his drawing, which showed an airplane with four heads sticking out of the windows.

She said, "I can understand that you drew three of the heads to show Joseph, Mary, and Jesus. But who's the fourth head?"

"Oh," answered the boy, "that's Pontius the pilot!"

Poor

There's one advantage in being poor—it's very inexpensive.

■ ■ ■

"How do you know your family was poor?"

"Every time I passed someone in town, they would say, 'There goes Joe. His poor family!'"

Poor Excuse

Jones came into the office an hour late for the third time in one week and found the boss waiting for him. "What's the story this time, Jones? Let's hear a good excuse for a change."

Jones sighed, "Everything went wrong this morning, Boss. My wife decided to drive me to the station.

She got ready in ten minutes, but then the drawbridge got stuck. Rather than let you down, I swam across the river (look, my suit is still damp), ran out to the airport, got a ride on Mr. Thompson's helicopter, landed on top of Radio City Music Hall, and was carried here piggyback by one of the Rockettes."

"You'll have to do better than that, Jones," said the boss. "No woman can get ready in ten minutes."

Popeye

A man sought medical aid because his eyes popped and his ears rang. A doctor looked him over and told him bluntly, "You've got six months to live." The doomed man decided he would treat himself right while he could. He bought a flashy car, hired a chauffeur, and retained the best tailor in town to make him 30 suits. He even decided his shirts would be made-to-order.

"Okay," said the tailor, "let's get your measurements. Hmm, thirty-five sleeve, sixteen collar—"

"Fifteen," the man said.

"Sixteen collar," the tailor repeated, measuring again.

"But I've always worn a fifteen collar," said the man.

"Listen," the tailor said, "I'm warning you, if you keep on wearing a fifteen collar, your eyes will pop and your ears will ring."

Porsche

A woman advertised a brand-new Porsche for sale for $10. A man answered the ad, but he was slightly disbelieving.

"What's the gimmick?" he inquired.

"No gimmick," the woman answered. "My husband died, and in his will he asked that the car be sold and the money go to his secretary."

Praise the Lord

Did you hear about the country parson who decided to buy himself a horse? The dealer assured him that the one he selected was a perfect choice. "This here horse has lived all his life in a religious atmosphere. So remember that he'll never start if you order, 'Giddyap.' You've got to say, 'Praise the Lord.' Likewise, a 'Whoa' will never make him stop. You've got to say, 'Amen.'"

Thus forewarned, the parson paid for the horse, mounted him, and with a cheery "Praise the Lord" set off for home. Suddenly, however, he noticed that the road ahead had been washed out, leaving a huge chasm. In a panic, he forgot his instructions and cried "Whoa" in vain several times. The horse just cantered on. At the very last moment he remembered to cry "Amen," and the horse stopped short at the very brink of the chasm. But that's when the parson, out of force of habit, murmured fervently, "Praise the Lord!"

Preaching

One Sunday a farmer went to church. When he entered he saw that he and the preacher were the only ones present. The preacher asked the farmer if he wanted him to go ahead and preach. The farmer said, "I'm not too smart, but if I went to feed my cattle and only one showed up, I'd feed him." So the minister began his sermon.

One hour passed, then two hours, and then two and a half hours. The preacher finally finished and came down to ask the farmer how he had liked the sermon.

The farmer answered slowly, "Well, I'm not very smart, but if I went to feed my cattle and only one showed up, I sure wouldn't feed him all the hay."

Prediction

Jim: If you're such a good fortune-teller, you should be able to tell me the score of tonight's hockey game before it starts.

Tim: Before the game starts, the score will be nothing to nothing.

President

Father: Son, do you realize when Lincoln was your age he was already studying hard to be a lawyer?

Son: Right, Pop, and when he was your age, he was already president of the United States.

Prize

Husband: The man who married my mother got a prize.

Wife: What was it?

Prodigal

A Sunday school class was being quizzed on the prodigal son. The teacher asked one youngster, "Who was sorry when the prodigal son returned home?"

The boy gave it a lot of deep thought and then said, "The fatted calf."

Prosperity

Few of us can stand prosperity—another man's, I mean.

Psychotics

Neurotics build air castles. Psychotics live in them. Psychiatrists collect the rent.

Punish

Woman: One of your bees just stung me. I want you to do something about it.

Beekeeper: Certainly, ma'am. Just show me which bee it was, and I'll have it punished.

Pursued

Deacon: It says here, "The wicked flee when no man pursueth."

Pastor: Yes, that's true, but they make much better time when somebody is after them.

Push

Mother: Did you push your little sister down the stairs?

Bobby: I only pushed her down one step. She fell the rest of the way.

■ ■ ■

A Baptist minister rushed down to the train station every single day to watch the Sunset Limited go by. There was no chore he wouldn't interrupt to carry out his ritual. Members of his congregation deemed his eccentricity juvenile and frivolous, and they asked him to give it up. "No, gentlemen," he said firmly. "I preach your sermons, teach your Sunday school, bury your dead, marry you, run your charities, and chair every drive it pleases you to conduct. I won't give up seeing that Southern Pacific train every day. I love it! It's the only thing in this town I don't have to push!"

Quaker Feeling His Oats

A burglar entered the house of a Quaker and proceeded to rob it. The Quaker heard noises, took his shotgun downstairs, and found the burglar. He aimed his gun and said gently, "Friend, I mean thee no harm, but thou standest where I am about to shoot."

Quick Thinking

A Scotsman and an Englishman were leaning against the counter in a store when a bandit walked in and brandished his gun.

The Scot, a quick thinker, hauled out his money and handed it to his English friend.

He said, "Here's the ten dollars you lent me."

Rain Checks

A visitor was engaged in conversation at the corner drugstore about the local drought.

"You think it's bad here," the merchant observed, "but down south o' here a-ways, they haven't had any rain for so long that the Baptists are sprinkling, the Methodists are using a damp cloth, and the Presbyterians are issuing rain checks!"

Raise

Employee: I've been here eleven years doing three men's work for one man's pay. I want a raise.

Boss: Well, I can't give you a raise, but if you'll tell me who the other two men are, I'll fire them.

Ralph

Myles: Suppose you loan Ralph ten dollars and he agrees to repay you at the rate of a dollar a week. How much money would you have after seven weeks?

Jay: Nothing.

Myles: Nothing? You don't know very much about math.

Jay: You don't know much about Ralph.

Rare Book

A collector of rare books ran into an acquaintance who had just thrown away an old Bible that had been in his family for generations. He happened to mention that Guten-something had printed it.

"Not Gutenberg?" gasped the book collector.

"Yes, that was the name."

"You idiot! You've thrown away one of the first books ever printed. A copy recently sold at an auction for millions!"

"Mine wouldn't have been worth a dime," replied the man. "Some clown by the name of Martin Luther had scribbled all over it."

Rash

A lady with a bad rash visited a dermatologist. She had suffered with the condition for some time.

"Have you been treated for this rash before?" inquired the doctor.

"Yes, by my druggist."

"And what sort of foolish advice did he give you?" asked the doctor.

"He told me to come and see you."

Real Safe

Wife: You know the old saying, "What you don't know won't hurt you"?

Husband: What about it?

Wife: You must really be safe.

A Real Turn-On

Did you hear about the Native American chief named Running Water? He had two daughters—Hot and Cold—and a son named Luke.

Reception Committee

About three weeks before an annual club dinner, a member received a letter from the club president, asking him to serve on the reception committee and to be there at seven o'clock sharp. A scarlet ribbon marked Reception Committee was enclosed. He hadn't intended to go because the dinners were usually a bore. But since he had been asked to be on the committee, he decided to go.

By the time he arrived, almost all 800 members of the club were there, each wearing a scarlet ribbon marked Reception Committee.

Refrigerator

A woman went to her psychiatrist and said, "Doctor, I want to talk to you about my husband. He thinks he's a refrigerator."

"That's not so bad," said the doctor. "It's a rather harmless complex."

"Well, maybe," replied the lady. "But he sleeps with his mouth open, and the light keeps me awake."

Remember

A worker was called on the carpet by his supervisor for talking back to his foreman. "Is it true that you called him a liar?"

"Yes, I did."

"Did you call him stupid?"

"Yes."

"Slave driver?"

"Yes."

"And did you call him an opinionated, bullheaded egomaniac?"

"No, but would you write that down so I can remember it?"

Repetition

Boss: The main thing to remember is that repetition, repetition, repetition is the key! If you have a product to sell, keep harping on it every possible way, cram it down people's throats...make yourself sickening and repulsive if you have to, but don't ever forget to repeat and repeat and repeat! It's the only way to get results!

Employee: Yes, sir.

Boss: And now, what was it you came in to see me about?

Employee: Well, sir, a raise! A raise! A raise! A raise! A raise! A raise! A raise! A raise…

Report Card

Here's my report card…and I'm tired of watching TV anyway.

Retail Store

Q. If a dog lost its tail, where would it get another one?

A. At the retail store.

Reverse Reason

She married him because he was such a "dominating man." She divorced him because he was such a "dominating male."

He married her because she was so "fragile and petite." He divorced her because she was so "weak and helpless."

She married him because "he knows how to provide a good living." She divorced him because "all he thinks about is business."

He married her because "she reminds me of my mother." He divorced her because "she's getting more like her mother every day."

She married him because he was "happy and

romantic." She divorced him because he was "shiftless and fun-loving."

He married her because she was "steady and sensible." He divorced her because she was "boring and dull."

She married him because he was "the life of the party." She divorced him because "he never wants to come home from a party."

Rich

Beverly: A scientist says that we become what we eat.
Melba: Oh, boy! Let's order something rich.

Rich Relative

Q. What type of person lives the longest?
A. A rich relative.

The Right Row

A man and his wife were running to their seats after a movie intermission. He asked a man at the end of a row, "Did I step on your toes on the way out?"

"You certainly did," responded the other angrily.

"All right," he said, turning to his wife. "This is our row."

Rip Van Winkle

A twentieth-century Rip Van Winkle slept for 20 years. Upon awaking he immediately found a telephone booth and called his broker.

"What's the stock market done the past twenty years?" he inquired.

His broker soon was able to report that his shares of AT&T were now worth $3 million, his shares of General Motors worth $2 million, and his oil holdings had increased to $4 million.

"Great!" Rip exclaimed. "I'm rich!"

A telephone operator interrupted and said, "Your three minutes are up, sir. Would you please deposit a million dollars?"

Road Maps

First husband: I think my wife is getting tired of me.

Second husband: What makes you feel that way?

First husband: She keeps wrapping my lunches in road maps.

Robbed

The teller had just been robbed for the third time by the same man, and the police officer was asking if he had noticed anything specific about the criminal.

"Yes," said the teller, "he seems to be better dressed each time."

Rock 'n' Roll

Ad in newspaper: "For sale cheap…my son's collection of rock 'n' roll records. If a boy's voice answers the phone, hang up and call later."

Rudolph

Mr. and Mrs. Smith were touring Russia. Their guide, a man named Rudolph, argued all the time. As the couple was leaving Moscow, the husband said, "Look, it's snowing out."

The guide disagreed, "No, sir, it's raining out."

"I still think it's snowing," said Mr. Smith.

But his wife replied, "Rudolph the Red knows rain, dear."

Rule the World

Husband: I know you are having a lot of trouble with the baby, dear, but keep in mind, "the hand that rocks the cradle rules the world."

Wife: How about taking over the world for a few hours while I go shopping?

Rumble, Rumble

An Army base staff was planning war games and didn't want to use live ammunition. Instead they informed the men, "In place of a rifle, say, 'Bang, bang.' In place of a knife, say, 'Stab, stab.' In place of a hand grenade, say, 'Lob, lob.'"

The games were in progress when one of the soldiers saw one of the enemy. He said, "Bang, bang," but nothing happened. He ran forward and said, "Stab, stab," but nothing happened. He ran back and went "Lob, lob," but nothing happened. Finally he walked up to the enemy and said, "You aren't playing fair. I said 'Bang,

bang,' 'Stab, stab,' and 'Lob, lob,' and you haven't fallen dead yet."

The enemy responded, "Rumble, rumble. I'm a tank."

Rumor

A flying rumor never has any trouble finding a place to land.

Sales, Not Management

An airliner flew into a violent thunderstorm and was soon swaying and bumping around the sky. One very nervous lady happened to be sitting next to a clergyman and turned to him for comfort.

"Can't you do something?" she demanded forcefully.

"I'm sorry, Ma'am," said the reverend gently. "I'm in sales, not management."

Salesman

A man walked into a men's clothing store and told the manager he wanted a job as a salesman.

"Sorry, we don't need any salesmen," the manager told him.

"But you've just got to hire me," the man said. "I'm the world's greatest salesman!"

The sales manager again refused, but the man hung on and was so convincing that finally the manager said, "Okay, I'll tell you what I'll do. See that suit over there hanging on the back wall? After you've dusted it off, you'll see that it has padded shoulders, pointed lapels, and a belt in the back. It's sort of a blue-orange-green-purple plaid. I don't even remember how I got stuck with it. Now, I'm going to lunch, and I'm going to leave you in charge. If you can sell that suit before I get back, you're hired."

About an hour later the manager returned to find the store in a mess. The rugs were ripped, a showcase was turned over, and merchandise was all over the floor, but the suit was gone.

"Well, I see you've sold the suit."

"Yes, sir."

"It looks like you had a little trouble with the customer though."

"No, sir. Not a bit of trouble with the customer—but oh, that seeing-eye dog."

Santa Claus

The four stages of man: He believes in Santa Claus, he does not believe in Santa Claus, he is Santa Claus, he looks like Santa Claus.

Sawmill

Ken: I slept like a log.
Melba: Yes, I heard the sawmill.

Scaffolding

Rob: My uncle fell off a scaffolding and was killed.
Bob: What was he doing up on the scaffolding?
Rob: Getting hanged.

Schoolteacher

A schoolteacher sent this note to all parents on the first day of school: "If you promise not to believe everything your child says happens at school, I'll promise not to believe everything he says happens at home."

Season Ticket

Todd: My wife just got a ticket for speeding.

Rod: That's nothing! My wife is so bad, the police gave her a season ticket.

Send the Bill

Doctor: I can do nothing for your sickness. It's hereditary.

Patient: Then send the bill to my father.

The Shirt off Your Back

A corporal reported to a new regiment with a letter from his old captain, saying, "This man is a great soldier, and he'll be even better if you can cure him of his constant gambling."

The new commanding officer looked at him sternly and said, "I hear you're an inveterate gambler. I don't approve. It's bad for discipline. What do you bet on?"

"Practically anything, sir," said the corporal. "If you'd like, I'll bet you a hundred dollars that you've got a strawberry birthmark under your right arm."

The CO snapped, "Put down your money." He then stripped to the waist, proved conclusively he had no birthmark, and pocketed the bills on the table. He couldn't wait to phone the captain and exult, "That corporal of yours won't be in a hurry to make a bet after what I just did to him."

"Don't be too sure," said the captain mournfully. "He just bet me a thousand bucks he'd get you to take your shirt off five minutes after he reported."

Shoe Repair

While rummaging through his attic, a man found a shoe-repair ticket that was nine years old. Figuring he had nothing to lose, he went to the shop and presented the ticket to the proprietor, who reluctantly began a search for the unclaimed shoes. After ten minutes, the owner reappeared and handed back the ticket.

"Well," asked the customer, "did you find the pair?"

"Yes," replied the shop owner. "They'll be ready Tuesday."

Shot

John: I shot my dog.

Don: Was he mad?

John: Well, it didn't seem to exactly please him.

Shower

A man once received a severe tongue-lashing from his wife. When he listened in silence, she was even more infuriated, so she picked up a pail of cold water and threw it over him, drenching him from head to foot.

With the water still dripping from him, very calmly

he remarked, "After that thunder and lightning, I rather expected a shower."

Sick Sack

My airplane flight was so rough that the stewards poured the food directly into the sick sacks!

Sign

Sign outside a house in the city: "Trespassers will be prosecuted to the full extent of one German shepherd."

· · ·

Outside a house in Sussex, England: "Beware of owner. Never mind the dog."

· · ·

Sign on garbage truck: "Satisfaction guaranteed or double your garbage back."

· · ·

Sally: What sign were you born under?
Beth: "Quiet—Hospital Zone."

Silence

Father: Did Paul bring you home last night?
Daughter: Yes—it was late, Daddy. Did the noise disturb you?
Father: No, my dear, it wasn't the noise. It was the silence.

Sin

A nice but blundering parishioner liked the new pastor and wanted to compliment him as she was leaving church after he had preached on sin. So she said to him, "I must say, sir, that we folks didn't know what sin was until you took charge of our parish."

Slow

"Look here, Private, this man beside you is doing twice the work you are."

"I know, Sarge. That's what I've been telling him for the last hour, but he won't slow down."

Slowly

Mr. and Mrs. McKee, vacationing in Rome, were touring the Colosseum.

"Now, this room," said the guide, "is where the slaves dressed to fight the lions."

"How does one dress to fight lions?" inquired Mr. McKee.

"Very slowly," replied the guide.

■ ■ ■

George was having trouble with a toothache, so he decided to visit the dentist. "What do you charge for extracting a tooth?" George asked.

"Fifty dollars," replied the dentist.

"Fifty dollars for only two minutes' work?" exclaimed George.

"Well," replied the dentist, "if you wish, I can extract it very slowly."

Small Humor

Q. How do you milk an ant?
A. First, you get a low stool...

Smart

Blow: Did you hear the smartest kid in the world is becoming deaf?
Joe: No, tell me about it.
Blow: What did you say?

Smile

To make a smile come, so they say,
brings 15 muscles into play.
But if you want a frown to thrive
you have to use some 65!

Smoking

Jay: Does the Bible say that if you smoke, you can't get to heaven?
Ray: No, but the more you smoke, the quicker you'll get there.

■ ■ ■

Did you hear about the man who read that smoking was bad for your health? He immediately gave up reading.

•••

Smoking a cigarette won't send you to hell. It just makes you smell as if you've been there.

Snoring

Why is it that the loudest snorer is always the first one to get to sleep?

So You Think You Have Troubles!

When I got to the building, I found that the hurricane had knocked some bricks off the top. So I rigged up a beam with a pulley at the top of the building and hoisted up a couple of barrels full of bricks. When I had fixed the building, there were a lot of bricks left over. Then I went to the bottom of the building and cast off the line. Unfortunately, the barrel of bricks was heavier than I was, and before I knew what was happening, the barrel started down, jerking me off the ground.

I decided to hang on, and halfway up I met the barrel coming down and received a hard blow on the shoulder. I then continued to the top, banging my head against the beam and getting my fingers jammed in the pulley. When the barrel hit the ground, it burst its bottom, allowing all the bricks to spill out.

I was now heavier than the barrel, so I started down again at high speed. Halfway down I met the barrel coming up and received more injuries to my shins.

When I hit the ground, I landed on the bricks, getting several painful cuts. At this point I must have lost my presence of mind because I let go the line. The barrel came down, giving me another heavy blow on the head and putting me in the hospital.

I respectfully request sick leave.

Soft Music

Some people ask the secret of our long marriage. We take time to go to a restaurant two times a week—a little candlelight dinner, soft music, and a slow walk home. She goes Tuesdays, and I go Fridays.

Some Can, Some Can't

The inmates of a prison had a joke book they all had memorized. They recited the jokes by the number of the joke. Some fellow would call out a number from one to one hundred, and all would laugh.

A new man in the prison, after studying the book, said he wanted to tell a joke. They said, "Okay, shoot!"

"Number twenty," he said, but nobody laughed.

He said, "This is funny. What's wrong—why aren't you laughing?"

A fellow nearby said, "Some can tell 'em, and some can't."

Son

One employee to another: "When the boss's son starts working here tomorrow, he'll have no special privileges or authority. Treat him just as you would anyone else who was due to take over the whole business in a year or two."

Speech

Upon entering a room in a hotel, a woman recognized a well-known government official pacing up and down, so she asked what he was doing there. "I am going to deliver a speech," he said.

"Do you usually get very nervous before addressing a large audience?"

"Nervous?" he replied. "No, I never get nervous."

"In that case," demanded the lady, "what are you doing in the ladies' room?"

■ ■ ■

Delivering a speech at a banquet on the night of his arrival in a large city, a visiting minister told several anecdotes he expected to repeat at meetings the next day. Because he wanted to use the jokes again, he requested that reporters omit them from any accounts they might turn in to their newspapers. A cub reporter, in commenting on the speech, ended his piece with this: "The minister told a number of stories that cannot be published."

Spit on You

I don't smoke, but I chew. Don't blow your smoke on me, and I won't spit on you.

Station

A janitor who worked in a railroad station decided to get married in a huge room on the upper floor of the station. So many friends and kinfolk showed up that their combined weight caused the building to collapse.

Moral of the story: Never marry above your station.

Stepping-Stones

Three men were in a boat halfway across a lake. The first man suddenly said, "I forgot my lunch." He got out of the boat and walked to shore on top of the water.

Later, the second man said, "I forgot my fishing tackle." He also walked across the water to shore.

By this time, the third man thought to himself, "They're not going to outsmart me. I forgot my bait can." He started to walk across the water, but he sank.

The first man said to the second, "Maybe we should have told him where the rocks were."

Stone

"My husband didn't leave a bit of insurance."

"Then where did you get that gorgeous diamond ring?"

"Well, he left a thousand for his casket and five thousand for a stone. This is the stone."

Stork

On his first visit to the zoo, a little boy stared at the caged stork for a long while. Then he turned to his father and exclaimed, "Gee, Dad, he doesn't recognize me."

■ ■ ■

Mother: What do you think of your new little brother, dear?

Brother: I wish we'd thrown him away and kept the stork instead.

St. Peter

An exasperated mother whose son was always getting into mischief finally asked him, "How do you expect to get into heaven?"

The boy thought it over and said, "Well, I'll just run in and out and in and out and keep slamming the door until St. Peter says, 'For heaven's sake, Jimmy, come in or stay out.'"

Story

We like the fellow who says he is going to make a long story short—and does.

Straight and Narrow

The dull thing about going down the straight and narrow path is that you so seldom meet anybody you know.

Straight Face

Father: When I was your age, I had never kissed a girl. Will you be able to tell your children that?

Son: Not with a straight face.

Stupid Idiot

Two men drove their cars toward each other on a narrow street—neither could pass. One leaned out and shouted, "I never back up for a stupid idiot!"

"I always do!" shouted the other man, shifting into reverse.

Success

They say success is 90 percent perspiration. You must be a tremendous success!

■ ■ ■

The road to success is dotted with many tempting parking spaces.

Sugar

Ben: One of our little pigs was sick, so I gave him some sugar.

Dan: Sugar! What for?

Ben: Haven't you ever heard of sugar-cured ham?

Sunday School

Son: Dad, did you go to Sunday school when you were young?

Dad: Never missed a Sunday.

Son: Bet it won't do me any good either.

Support

Father: Can you support her in the way she's been accustomed to?

Prospective son-in-law: No, but I can support her in the way her mother was accustomed to when she first married.

Sure Thing

"If you refuse to marry me, I'll die," said the young romantic. And sure enough, 50 years later, he died.

Surly

Cheerful people, the doctors say, resist disease better than the glum ones. In other words, the surly bird catches the germ.

Swap

A tribal chieftain's daughter was offered as a bride to the son of a neighboring potentate in exchange for two cows and four sheep. The big swap was to be effected on the shore of the stream that separated the two tribes. Pop and his daughter showed up at the appointed time, only to discover that the groom and his livestock were on the other side of the stream. The father grunted, "The fool doesn't know which side his bride is bartered on."

The System

Advertising manager: Where did you get this wonderful follow-up system? It would drag money out of anybody.

Assistant: I'll say it would. It's compiled from the letters my son wrote me from college.

Tact

Social tact is making your company feel at home even though you wish they were.

Take It Slow

A bachelor kept a cat for companionship and loved it more than life. He was planning a trip to England and entrusted the cat to his brother's care.

As soon as he arrived in England, he called his brother. "How is my cat?" he asked.

"Your cat is dead," came the reply.

"Oh my," he exclaimed. "Did you have to tell me that way?"

"How else can I tell you your cat's dead?" inquired the brother.

"You should have led me up to it gradually," said the bachelor. "For example, when I called tonight you could have told me my cat was on the roof, but the fire department is getting it down. When I called tomorrow night, you could have told me they dropped him and broke his back, but a fine surgeon is doing all he can for him. Then, when I called the third night, you could have told me the surgeon did all he could but my cat passed away. That way it wouldn't have been such a shock. By the way," he continued, "how's Mother?"

"Mother?" came the reply. "Oh, she's up on the roof, but the fire department is getting her down."

Take the Books

The burglars had tied and gagged the bank cashier after extracting the combination to the safe and had herded the other employees into a separate room under guard. After they rifled the safe and were about to leave, the cashier made desperate pleading noises through the gag. Moved by curiosity, one of the burglars loosed the gag.

"Please," whispered the cashier, "take the books too. I'm a few hundred dollars short."

Take Two Aspirin

A doctor had a problem with a leak in his bathroom plumbing that became bigger and bigger. Even though it was two a.m., the doctor decided to phone his plumber.

"For Pete's sake, Doc," he wailed, "this is some time to wake a guy."

"Well," the doctor answered testily, "you've never hesitated to call me in the middle of the night with a medical problem. Now it just happens I've got a plumbing emergency."

There was a moment's silence. Then the plumber

spoke up, "Right you are, Doc," he agreed. "Tell me what's wrong."

The doctor explained about the leak in the bathroom.

"Tell you what to do," the plumber offered. "Every four hours, drop two aspirin down the pipe. If the leak hasn't cleared up by morning, phone me at the office."

Take-Out Service

Passenger: Stewardess, this is the worst steak I ever had. I'm sending it back—bring me another one!

Stewardess: Will that be to take out?

Talking Dog

A man tried to sell his neighbor a new dog. "This is a talking dog," he said. "And you can have him for five dollars."

The neighbor said, "Who do you think you're kidding with this talking-dog stuff? There's no such animal."

Suddenly the dog looked up with tears in his eyes. "Please buy me, sir," he pleaded. "This man is cruel. He never buys me a meal, never bathes me, never takes me for a walk. And I used to be the richest trick dog in America. I performed before kings. I was in the Army and was decorated ten times."

"Hey!" said the neighbor. "He can talk. Why do you want to sell him for just five dollars?"

"Because," said the seller, "I'm getting tired of all his lies."

Tax Collector

A man walked into the IRS office, sat down, and smiled at everyone.

"May I help you?" said the clerk in charge.

"No, thank you," said the man. "I just wanted to meet the people I've been working for all these years."

Taxes

April 15 should be called Taxgiving Day.

Tea

Three Englishmen stopped at a restaurant for a spot of tea. The waiter appeared with pad and pencil.

"I'll have a glass of weak tea," ordered the first.

"I'll have tea too," said the second, "but very strong with two pieces of lemon."

"Tea for me too, please," said the third. "But be sure the glass is absolutely clean."

In a short time the waiter was back with the order. "All right," he asked "Which one gets the clean glass?"

Teenagers

"What did your teenage daughter do all summer?"

"Her hair and her nails."

■ ■ ■

Father to teenage son: "Do you mind if I use the car tonight? I'm taking your mother out and I would like to impress her."

■ ■ ■

Dad: Did you use the car last night?
Son: Yes—I took some of the boys for a ride.
Dad: Well, tell them I found two of their lipsticks.

■ ■ ■

Father: I want you home by eleven.
Teenage daughter: But Daddy, I'm no longer a child.
Father: I know. That's why I want you home by eleven.

■ ■ ■

If you live in a house full of teenagers, it is not necessary to ask for whom the bell tolls. It's not for you.

Teeth

There are three basic rules for having good teeth:

1. Brush them twice a day.

2. See your dentist twice a year.

3. Keep your nose out of other people's business.

Temptation

A driver tucked this note under the windshield wiper of his automobile. "I've circled the block for 20 minutes. I'm late for an appointment, and if I don't park here I'll lose my job. 'Forgive us our trespasses.'"

When he came back he found a parking ticket and

this note: "I've circled the block for 20 years, and if I don't give you a ticket, I'll lose my job. 'Lead us not into temptation.'"

Texas

An Easterner was riding with a rancher over a blistering and almost barren stretch of West Texas when a strange bird scurried in front of them. The Easterner asked what the bird was, and the rancher replied, "That's a bird of paradise."

The stranger from the East rode on in silence for a moment and then said, "Long way from home, isn't it?"

That's My Speech

Chauncey Depew once played a trick on Mark Twain when they both spoke at a banquet. Twain spoke first for some 20 minutes and was received with great enthusiasm. When Depew's turn came immediately afterward, he said, "Mr. Toastmaster, ladies and gentlemen, before this dinner, Mark Twain and I made an agreement to trade speeches. He has just delivered mine, and I'm grateful for the reception you have accorded it. I regret that I have lost his speech and cannot remember a thing he had to say."

He sat down with much applause.

That's Once

A couple was celebrating their golden wedding anniversary. Their domestic tranquility had long been the talk of the town. A local newspaper reporter inquired as to the secret of their long and happy marriage.

"Well, it dates back to our honeymoon," explained the lady. "We visited the Grand Canyon and took a trip down to the bottom of the canyon on mules. We hadn't gone too far when my husband's mule stumbled. My husband took the mule by the ears, shook him vigorously and said 'That's once.' We proceeded a little farther, and the mule stumbled again. Once more my husband took him by the ears, shook him even more vigorously and said, 'That's twice.' We hadn't gone half a mile before the mule stumbled a third time. My husband promptly removed a revolver from his pocket and shot him.

"I started to protest over his treatment of the mule, but he grabbed me by the ears, shook me vigorously, and said 'That's once.'"

Theophilus

When he was born, the doctor called him Theophilus. He's The Awfullest baby I have ever seen.

Theories

Fifteen years ago, I had six theories about parenting but no children. Now I have six children and no theories.

Thoughtful

A tightwad was looking for a gift for a friend. Everything was too expensive except for a glass vase that had been broken. He asked the store to send it, hoping his friend would think it had been broken in transit.

In due time he received an acknowledgment: "Thanks for the vase. It was so thoughtful of you to wrap each piece separately."

Three-Headed Monster

A little boy came home from school crying, "Mommy, Mommy! The kids at school called me a three-headed monster."

The mother responded sympathetically: "Now, there, there, there."

Tiny Chuckles

Q. What is a small joke called?
A. A mini ha ha.

Title

In an age when everyone seems to be playing the name game of glorifying job titles, the man in charge of the meat department at a store in Wichita Falls, Texas, deserves a round of applause. On his weekly time card he describes his position as Meat Head.

Tomorrow

Ken: There's nothing like getting up at five in the morning for a five-mile jog and an ice-cold shower before breakfast.

Bob: How long have you been doing this?

Ken: I start tomorrow.

■ ■ ■

"Remember our vacation, when we spent money like there was no tomorrow? Well, it's tomorrow."

Tongue

Once when C.H. Spurgeon, then a young man, was passing by the house of a woman with a poison tongue, she let him have a volley of impolite words. "Yes, thank you; I am quite well," Spurgeon said. Then she let out another volley. "Yes, it does look as if it's going to rain," he replied.

Surprised, the woman exclaimed, "That man's deaf as a post! What's the use of talking to him?"

Top This

Bill: My dog swallowed a tapeworm and died by inches.

Bob: That's nothing—my dog crawled up in my bed and died by the foot.

Ken: I can beat that. I had a dog that went out of the house and died by the yard.

Traffic Fine

"What am I supposed to do with this?" grumbled the motorist as the police clerk handed him a receipt for his traffic fine.

"Keep it," the clerk advised. "When you get four of them, you get a bicycle."

Train

On a visit to tiny Israel, a Texan boasted: "Why, in Texas you can get on a train, ride for days, and still be in Texas."

His Israeli companion nodded sympathetically.

"We have the same trouble with our trains," he said.

Train of Thought

Abe: Be quiet, please. You're interrupting my train of thought.

Gabe: Let me know when it comes to a station.

Train Ride

Mark Twain once encountered a friend at the races who said, "I'm broke. Will you buy me a ticket back to town?"

Twain said, "Well, I'm pretty broke myself, but I'll tell you what to do. You hide under my seat, and I'll cover you with my legs." The friend agreed, and Twain then went to the ticket office and bought two tickets. When the train was underway and the supposed stowaway was snug under the seat, the conductor came by, and Twain gave him the two tickets.

"Where is the other passenger?" asked the conductor.

Twain tapped on his forehead and said in a loud voice, "That is my friend's ticket. He is a little eccentric and likes to ride under the seat."

Train to Buffalo

An executive in New York boarded a train to Chicago. He explained to the porter, "I'm a heavy sleeper, and I want you to be sure and wake me at three a.m. to get off in Buffalo. Regardless of what I say, get me up, for I have some important business there."

The next morning he awakened in Chicago. He found the porter and really poured it on with abusive language.

After he had left, someone said, "How could you stand there and take that kind of talk from that man?"

The porter said, "That's nothing. You should have heard the man I put off in Buffalo."

Trumpet

A man complained to his landlord about the upstairs tenants. "They often stamp on the floor and shout till midnight."

When the landlord asked if it bothered him, he replied, "Not really. I usually stay up and practice my trumpet till about that time anyway."

Trying

Mother, having finally tucked her small boy into bed after an unusually trying day: "Well, I've worked today from son-up to son-down!"

Turkey

Husband: That's a beautiful Thanksgiving turkey! What kind of stuffing did you use?

Wife: This one wasn't hollow!

Turnabout Is Fair Play

Two girls boarded a crowded bus, and one of them whispered to the other, "Watch me embarrass a man into giving me his seat."

Pushing her way through the crowd, she turned all her charms on a gentleman who looked like he might embarrass easily. "My dear Mr. Wilson," she gushed, "fancy meeting you on the bus. Am I glad to see you. Why, you're almost a stranger. My, but I'm tired."

The sedate gentleman looked up at the girl. He had never seen her before, but he rose and said pleasantly, "Sit down, Mary, my girl. It isn't often I see you on laundry day. No wonder you're tired. Being pregnant isn't easy. By the way, don't deliver the wash until Thursday. My wife is going to the district attorney's office to see whether she can get your husband out of jail."

Tweedle

A minister named Tweedle reluctantly refused a doctor of divinity degree. He said that he'd rather be Tweedle dumb than Tweedle DD.

Twins

Melba: I guess your husband was pleased when he found out you were having twin boys.

Pam: Was he! He went around grinning from heir to heir.

Unbelievable

A man rose from his seat in a crowded bus so a lady standing nearby could sit down. She was so surprised that she fainted.

When she revived and sat down, she said, "Thanks." Then he fainted.

Vacation

A period of travel and relaxation when you take twice the clothes and half the money you need.

* * *

If you can't get away for a vacation, just tip every third person you meet, and you'll get the same effect.

Vending Machine

A man put a coin in a vending machine and watched helplessly while the cup failed to appear. One nozzle sent coffee down the drain while another poured cream after it.

"Now that's real automation!" he exclaimed. "It even drinks for you!"

A Very Sensitive Dog

Did you hear about the dog who played Bach? He was about to be auditioned by a TV producer. The dog's agent warned the producer that this was a very sensitive dog. "You had better listen to him play because if you don't, he loses his temper and leaps at you."

The dog started to play. He was awful. The TV producer patiently waited out the performance. When it was over, he declared angrily, "I should have let him attack. I'm sure his Bach is worse than his bite."

Veterinarian

A rancher asked a veterinarian for some free advice. "I have a horse that sometimes walks normally and sometimes he limps. What shall I do?"

The veterinarian replied, "The next time he walks normally, sell him."

Voice

The choir had finished a rehearsal.

"Do you do a lot of singing at home?" Bill asked a fellow choir member.

"Yes, I sing a lot. I use my voice just to kill time," Roy replied.

Bill nodded. "You certainly have a fine weapon."

Waiter

Diner: Is it customary to tip the waiter in this restaurant?

Waiter: Why...ah...yes, sir.

Diner: Then hand me a tip. I've waited almost an hour for my steak.

Wallet

Did you hear about the man who went carp fishing? As he was about to throw his first cast, his wallet fell out of his pocket and into the lake. A carp grabbed the wallet and started to swim away with it. Suddenly, another carp ate the carp that had eaten the wallet. Then yet another even larger carp came along and swallowed the carp that ate the carp that devoured the wallet.

And that's how carp-to-carp walleting began.

Watch the First Step

Q. How can you jump off a 50-foot ladder and not get hurt?

A. Jump off the first step.

We Like It

A fellow had been standing in line to get into a movie theater. When he reached the box office, he was surprised to see that the ticket price was $10. He pointed to a sign that said "Popular Prices" and said, "You call ten dollars 'popular'?"

"We like it," answered the girl sweetly.

Weather

Everybody talks about the weather, but nobody does anything about it.

■ ■ ■

Don't knock the weather. Nine-tenths of the population couldn't start a conversation if the weather didn't change once in a while.

Weep and Sniffle

Husband: Why do you weep and sniffle over a TV program and the imaginary woes of people you've never met?

Wife: For the same reason you scream and yell when a man you don't know makes a touchdown.

Weevils

Two boll weevils came from the country to the city. One became rich and famous. The other remained the lesser of the two weevils.

Weight

If you really want to lose weight, there are only three things you must give up: breakfast, lunch, and dinner.

Weight Lifter

A weight lifter was boasting about his strength and went on about it for some time. A gardener overheard and made him this offer: "Tell you what. I'll bet you twenty-five bucks I can wheel a load in this wheelbarrow over there to the other side of the street that you can't wheel back."

"You're on," said the weight lifter. "What's your load going to be?"

"Get in," said the gardener.

Well Done

Husband: "How do you want the electric blanket tonight, dear—rare, medium or well done?"

Well Informed

You can always tell when a man is well informed. His views are pretty much like your own.

What a Dream

Wife: I dreamed you gave me two hundred dollars for summer clothes last night. You wouldn't spoil that dream, would you, dear?

Husband: Of course not, darling. You can keep the money.

What a Finnish

Finn and Huck were lifelong friends. When Finn died, everyone said, "Huck'll bury Finn."

What a Mess

A college boy said to his mother, "I've decided to be a political science major and clean up the mess in the world."

"That's very nice," purred his mother. "You can go upstairs and start with your room."

What a Relief

A man, fond of practical jokes, late one night sent his friend a collect telegram that read, "I am perfectly well."

A week later the joker received a heavy parcel on which he had to pay considerable charges. He opened it and found a big block of concrete on which was pasted this message: "This is the weight your telegram lifted from my mind."

What a Tail

A man was waiting at an intersection for a circus to pass by. He saw a sign on one of the wagons that read, "Barney's Circus with 50 Elephants." He counted the elephants as they crossed the intersection. When he got to 50, he put his car in gear and started to cross the intersection because he was late for an appointment. Unfortunately, he had miscounted, and his car hit and killed the last elephant.

A week later he got a notice from the circus that he'd have to pay $200,000. He called the circus manager and inquired, "What's the deal? I only hit one lousy elephant! Why do you want two hundred thousand?"

The manager responded, "It's true, you only hit one elephant, but you pulled the tails out of forty-nine others!"

What a Wreck

Two truck drivers applied for a job. One said, "I'm Pete, and this is my partner, Mike. When I drive at night, he sleeps."

The man said, "All right, I'll give you an oral test. It's three in the morning. You're on a one-lane bridge, and your truck is loaded with nitroglycerin. Suddenly a truck comes toward you at about eighty miles an hour. What's the first thing you do?"

"I wake up my partner, Mike. He's never seen a wreck like this before."

What a Year

Melba: My husband was named Man of the Year.

Pam: Well, that shows you what kind of a year it's been.

What's the Big Deal?

Little Billy was left to fix lunch. When his mother returned with a friend, she noticed that Billy had already strained the tea.

"Did you find the tea strainer?" his mother asked.

"No, Mother, I couldn't, so I used the fly swatter," replied Billy.

His mother nearly fainted, so Billy hastily added, "Don't get excited, Mother. I used an old one."

Where's My Cat?

"Hello, police department? I've lost my cat and—"

"Sorry, sir, that's not a job for the police. We're too busy—"

"But you don't understand. This is a very intelligent cat. He's almost human. He can practically talk."

"Well, you'd better hang up, sir. He may be trying to phone you right now."

Where's My Parakeet?

A carpet layer had worked all day installing wall-to-wall carpeting. When he noticed a lump under the carpet in the middle of the living room, he felt his shirt pocket for his cigarettes—they were gone. He was not about to take up the carpet, so he went outside for a two-by-four. Stamping down cigarettes with it would be easy. Once the lump was smoothed, the man gathered up his tools and carried them to the truck. Then two things happened simultaneously. He saw his cigarettes on the seat of the truck, and over his shoulder he heard the voice of the woman to whom the carpet belonged: "Have you seen my parakeet?"

Who Listens?

Two eminently successful psychoanalysts occupied offices in the same building. One was 40 years old, the other more than 70. They rode on the elevator together at the end of an unbearably hot, sticky day. The younger man was completely done in, and he noted with some resentment that his senior was fresh as a daisy. "I don't understand," he marveled. "How can you listen to drooling patients from morning till night on a day like this and still look so spry and unbothered when it's over?"

The older analyst said simply, "Who listens?"

Whom Do I Shoot?

A new soldier was on sentry duty at the main gate of a military outpost. His orders were clear: No car was to enter unless it had a special sticker on the windshield. A big Army car came up with a general seated in the back. The sentry said, "Halt, who goes there?"

The chauffeur, a corporal, said, "General Wheeler."

"I'm sorry, I can't let you through. You've got to have a sticker on the windshield."

The general said, "Drive on."

The sentry said, "Hold it. You really can't come through. I have orders to shoot if you try driving in without a sticker."

The general repeated, "I'm telling you, son, drive on."

The sentry walked up to the rear window and said, "General, I'm new at this. Do I shoot you or the driver?"

Who's That Woman?

Wife: This article on overpopulation says that somewhere in the world, every four seconds a woman is having a baby.

Husband: Someone ought to find that woman and stop her!

Who's There?

Wife: A man at the door wants to see you about a bill you owe him. He wouldn't give his name.

Husband: What does he look like?

Wife: He looks like you'd better pay him.

A Whole Hour

One day an employee arrived late with one eye closed, his left arm in a sling, and his clothes in tatters. "It's nine thirty," pointed out the president. "You're an hour late."

The employee explained, "I fell out of a tenth-story window."

The president snorted. "It took you a whole hour?"

Will

A rich man died, and a line in his will read as follows: "I leave to my beloved nephew all the money he owes me."

Wind

A tourist traveling through western Kansas saw a man sitting by the ruins of a house that had been blown away.

"Was this your house, my friend?" he asked sympathetically.

"Yep."

"Any of your family blown away with the house?"

"Yes, my wife and four kids."

"Good heavens! Why aren't you hunting for them?"

"Well, I've been in this country quite a spell. The wind's due to change this afternoon. I figure I might as well wait here till it brings 'em back."

Wiped Out

The most embarrassing moment in the life of Jane Wyman happened when she was entertaining very special guests. After looking over all the arrangements carefully, she wrote a note to her husband and put it on the guest towels. "If you use these, I will murder you."

In all her preparations, she forgot to remove the note. After the guests departed, the towels were discovered still in perfect order, as well as the note itself.

Wits

Bill: I have had to make a living by my wits.
Gill: Well, half a living is better than none.

Wondering

We have a strange and wonderful relationship. He's strange and I'm wonderful.

Wooden Leg

Fred: There is a man outside with a wooden leg named Martin.
Jed: What is the name of his other leg?

Wool

A man who owned many sheep wanted to take them over a frozen river, but the woman who owned the river said no. So he promised to marry her, and that's how he pulled the wool over her ice.

Worry

Red: I'd give a thousand dollars to anyone who would do my worrying for me.
Ted: You're on. Where's the thousand?
Red: That's your first worry.

Wrecked

Pretty young girl to friend: "Not only has Jack broken my heart and wrecked my whole life, but he has spoiled my entire evening!"

Wrong Again

Husband: We've been married five years and haven't agreed on a thing.

Wife: Wrong again. It's been six years.

Young Woman

The seven ages of a woman are baby, child, girl, young woman, young woman, young woman, and poised social leader.

Your Problem—My Situation

When you get angry, it's because you are ill-tempered. It just happens that my nerves are bothering me.

When you don't like someone, it's because you are prejudiced. I happen to be a good judge of human nature.

When you compliment someone, it's because you use flattery. I only encourage folks.

When you take a long time to do a job, it's because you are unbearably slow. When I take a long time, it's because I believe in quality workmanship.

When you spend your paycheck in 24 hours, it's because you are a spendthrift. When I do, it's because I'm generous.

When you stay in bed until 11 a.m., it's because you're a lazy good-for-nothing. When I stay in bed a little longer, it's because I'm totally exhausted.

Zipper

Q. How do you make an elephant fly?

A. Well, first you take a grea-a-t big zipper...

More Fun
Harvest House Books
by Bob Phillips

For more information about Bob Phillips' books,
send a self-addressed stamped envelope to:

Family Services
P.O. Box 9363
Fresno, California 93702